We to   to the hills!

D0119770

Joly

THE MIDDLE MARCHES

Ludlow Castle, for nearly two centuries the royal seat from which all the Marcher counties and Wales were governed

THE MIDDLE MARCHES

Between Severn and Wye

by HARRY BAKER

with illustrations by MIKE MORRIS

ROBERT HALE · LONDON

© *Text Harry Baker 1983*
© *Illustrations Mike Morris 1983*
First published in Great Britain 1983

ISBN 0 7090 0923 2

Robert Hale Limited
Clerkenwell House
Clerkenwell Green
London EC1R 0HT

Photoset in Palatino by
Kelly Typesetting Limited
Bradford-on-Avon, Wiltshire
Printed in Great Britain by
Redwood Burn Limited
Trowbridge, Wiltshire
Bound by W.B.C. Bookbinders Limited

Contents

CONTENTS

COMPANION VOLUMES

Heart of England by Louise Wright and James Priddey
Rural Kent by John Boyle and John L. Berbiers
Cotswold Heritage by Louise Wright and James Priddey
Sussex Scenes by Michael H. C. Baker
Somerset Scenes by Aylwin Sampson
A Picture of Surrey by John L. Baker

Acknowledgement

Acknowledgement is made to the Society of Authors as
the literary representative of the Estate of A. E. Housman
and to Jonathan Cape Ltd for permission to quote from
A. E. Housman's *Collected Poems*.

Illustrations

ILLUSTRATIONS

*To all my family and friends who helped
— but to my wife most of all*

Introduction

Between the River Severn and Offa's Dyke lies a country-side of ever-changing charm, where hills with the out-lines of mountains tower over fertile meadows, where timber and tile complement brick and stone, and where wild flowers star high-banked lanes resonant with bird-song.

It is the land of which the old jingle sings: 'Happy the eye between Severn and Wye' and A. E. Housman of *A Shropshire Lad* wrote 'the smooth green miles of turf' and the wind blowing 'the saplings double' on Wenlock Edge; where the seas of wild daffodils wrung rhymes from Ledbury-born Poet Laureate John Masefield; and memories of which made Worcester's novelist Francis Brett Young pine in exile and compose a history in verse called *The Island*, with a 'Song of the Three Rivers'.

He was hymning the Severn, the longest river in Britain (220 miles, ten more than the Thames) and its two main tributaries, the Teme from the west and the Warwickshire Avon from the east.

To explore it we started from where the Severn plunges into the spectacular gorge the Ice Age forced it to cut at Ironbridge, then followed it to Tewkesbury, the highest point reached by the famous Bore and so nearing the estuary and salt-water. We made our southern boundary the motorway M50 to Ross, where we took the course of the Wye's tributary, the Monnow, as it forms both Herefordshire's southern boundary and that between England and Wales. At the southern edge of the Black Mountains, from which the Monnow gushes, we began the return along the line of the Offa's Dyke Path topping the two-thousand-feet-high escarpment, then continued along it as it crosses the valleys of the rivers coming from Wales with a small market town at each junction – the Wye at Hay, the Arrow at Kington, the Lugg at Presteigne, the Teme at Knighton and the Clun at Clun. Then we struck across the Shropshire Highlands back to the Severn Gorge.

Most of the country inside the great noose we arbitrarily cast comes within the Diocese of Hereford that Offa set up about the time he built his 168-mile-long dyke. An idea of its size came during the pilgrimage the Bishop of Hereford made in 1982 when he walked some two hundred miles visiting his parishes. That does not cover the Vale of Evesham and the fringes of the Severn, which are in the Diocese of Worcester.

Man has long been marking his presence in this land where hills with the spirit and shape of mountains rear distinctive outlines from fertile well-watered valleys. In the Stone Age traders in flints and stone axes used the hilltops where thousands of years later Iron Age tribesmen prepared camps in an attempt to hold back the Romans building colonizing roads in the valleys. Saxons built on sites that the Normans later expanded for their castles, churches and planned towns. By Tudor times massive oak beams were being used more and more. As locally made brick became increasingly plentiful, great and gracious Jacobean, Queen Anne and Georgian houses went up. And before modern building methods settled, the opulent Victorian styles erupted.

Examples of all these are plentiful inside our noose, with the half-timbered 'magpies' especially striking. Conservation as a fine art stepped in before the shopping-precinct entrepreneurs could wipe out the heritage – except for the two cathedral cities of Worcester and Hereford, and to a lesser extent the abbey town of Tewkesbury. So market towns like Ludlow and Ledbury, Pershore and Much Wenlock, Bromyard and Ross,

remain unspoilt at their hearts in spite of the rumbles of heavy traffic.

Nearly all have had their moments in history, and some have many to remember, because this peaceful land was not so tranquil in the past. Here the Romans fought the Britons, the Saxons the Welsh, the Danes and later the Normans. The Marcher lords fought not only the Welsh but each other and even the King, with the Mortimers coming to the top of the pack to become the Earls of March and the Yorkist kings of England. There is Mortimer blood in the royal family through Elizabeth of York's marriage to Henry VII which united the Lancastrians and Yorkists in the red-and-white Tudor Rose. And in the Civil War struggle between King and Parliament, the natural defence the Severn gave made this a major Royalist bastion, with both the first skirmish and the final battle at Worcester – and the local people the prey of each side.

The countryside also has its protectors, The National Trust owns large areas, particularly of hill-walking, and tracks run through vast areas of Forestry Commission woodland, notably on the actual border. Much of the land is scheduled as being of outstanding natural beauty, particularly in South Shropshire, where eighty per cent of 250,000 acres is so scheduled. The charm of the Marches' 'infinite variety', to quote Shakespeare (although he was describing Cleopatra) ranges from the plump comfort of the Vale of Evesham and the Bredon

Hill villages to the starkly etched profile of the east face of the Black Mountains, from the fossilized hive of industry in the Severn Gorge to the hopfields and orchards of Herefordshire where the colours of soil and cattle match.

The intricate pattern of minor roads and lanes is like that G. K. Chesterton wrote about – 'Before the Roman . . . on to Severn strode, the rolling English drunkard made the rolling English road'. Perhaps the hops and apples stirred even the austere Housman when he untypically wrote:

O many a peer of England brews
Livelier liquor than the Muse,
And malt does more than Milton can
To justify God's ways to Man.

Even before the Real Ale campaign began, home-brewed beer persisted in such places as Bishop's Castle against the competition of the big brewers and Hereford's concern with cider is such that a cider-press is used as an eye-catcher near a roundabout on its ring road.

The great composer Elgar was brought up at Worcester, lived for years at Hereford and is buried at Malvern, where works he created included *The Dream of Gerontius*. This, too, is the land of the Three Choirs Festival, alternating each year between Worcester, Hereford and Gloucester.

Langland wrote his medieval *Vision of Piers Plowman* on Malvern Hills and Milton his masque *Comus* at Ludlow Castle. The Rev. Francis Kilvert's diary recorded his Victorian life in the middle section of the Wye Valley. Mary Webb created her novels in the Shropshire Highlands where in the post-Second World War years Malcolm Saville set his children's *Lonely Pine Club* adventure stories. The American poet Robert Frost settled with kindred spirits in the daffodil land on the Herefordshire/Gloucestershire border.

The land around which we threw our noose is one to sing about and we enjoyed every minute and every mile we spent exploring it. We hope you do, too.

Harry Baker and Mike Morris

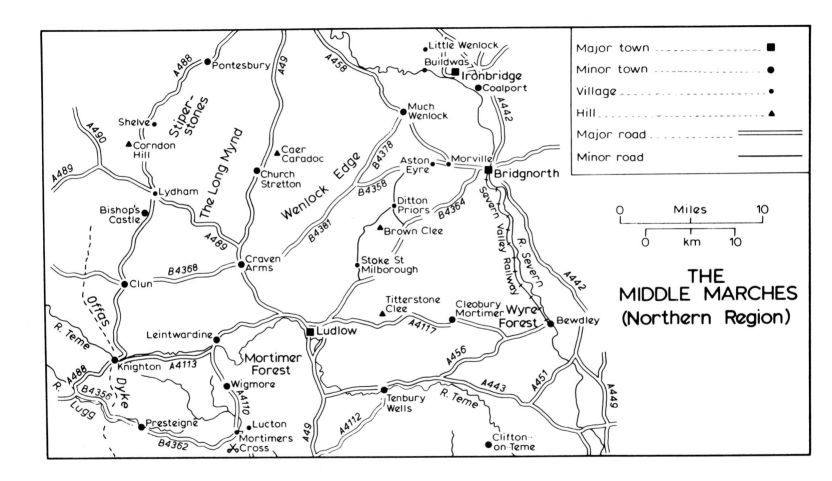

THE
MIDDLE MARCHES
(Northern Region)

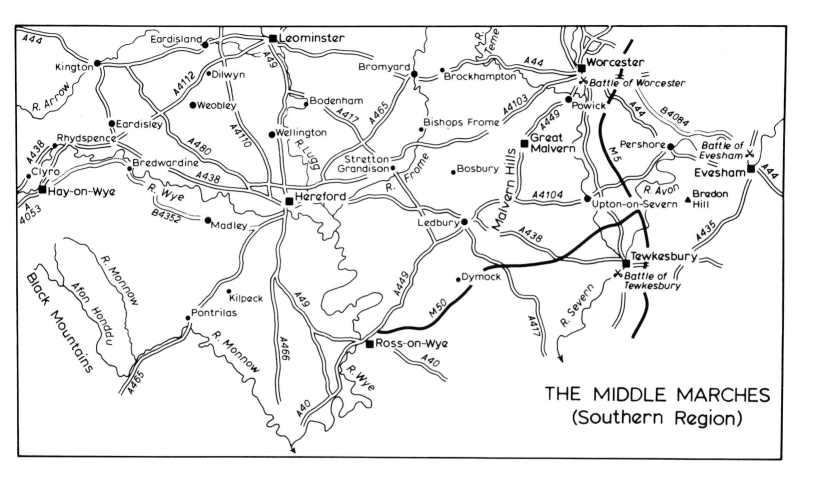

THE MIDDLE MARCHES
(Southern Region)

CHAPTER ONE

Where It All Started

When spring thaws or summer storms send incalculable amounts of floodwater hurtling out of mid-Wales the Severn, red-brown with the soil it has clawed from its flanks, tears frightening and ferocious below the oldest iron bridge in the world on its way to the Bristol Channel and the sea.

To stand on the bridge and peer through the lattice-work into the maelstrom below is as terrifying as a close-up view of a frothing, snarling tiger through the bars of its cage. But the mundane fact at the root of the bridge's creation is that three centuries ago a young man discovered that he could cast three-legged cooking pots (the type cannibals are supposed to have used for missionaries) from iron instead of brass.

Two years later the same young man made another discovery, which started the Industrial Revolution, in Shropshire at a spot only a few hundred yards upriver of the bridge. His name was Abraham Darby. He was a Quaker born at Sedgley, Staffordshire, who had been apprenticed to a Birmingham firm specializing in making mills for malt. He set up a business of his own at Briston, manufacturing brass wire and later cooking pots, before a visit to Holland gave him the idea of casting pots of iron, thinner and lighter than thought possible.

He decided to move, to get his raw materials more easily and cheaply, to Coalbrookdale in Shropshire, where the Severn gouges a deep gorge through layers of coal and limestone, iron-ore and clay. That was back in 1707 and Abraham Darby was 29. Two years later he made the breakthrough that changed the face of iron-making – and Western civilization. He remembered that during his Birmingham apprenticeship coke, part-burnt coal, had been used in making malt. Why not try it for iron-making instead of charcoal, part-burnt wood? He and his workmen did – and it worked. Later his successors found that by adding the abundant limestone to raw coal, there was no need to go through the coke-making process. The Severn Gorge boomed with trade and noise, bustle and growth. The Industrial Revolution was under way.

Ironbridge houses climbing up the steep slopes from Wharfside looking upriver from the iron bridge

But by the end of the eighteenth century a snag had been encountered. It was dangerous and uneconomic to be limited to boats to keep crossing the Severn, the highway on which the trade depended. So they decided to bridge it, using the new 'in' metal, iron. The old furnace of the first Abraham Darby was dug out in 1959 (to mark the 250th anniversary of his discovery) from beneath fourteen thousand tons of slag and old buildings by its owners, still with Darby connections. Now it is one of the pioneer sites administered by the Ironbridge Gorge Museum Trust, which preserves historic industrial sites in a three-mile stretch of the gorge with the kind of pride that old-fashioned Prussian officers bestowed on the duelling scars on their cheeks.

The Trust received a major award in 1977 for its presentation of its properties, more than half-a-dozen in all, and an international award the following year. For each of them there is a printed guide, well-presented and good value.

On the south bank of the iron bridge is the toll-house, which was given a face-lift before being opened by Billy Wright, the former Wolverhampton Wanderers and England football captain, who must be the gorge's most famous sportsman, excepting possibly the celebrated Captain Matthew Webb, the first to swim the English Channel (in August 1875), who was born in what later became Ironbridge's police station.

The toll-house has a recorded television commentary and photographs of what has been done to make the bridge safe. Since 1931 only pedestrians have been allowed to use it, but an old painted panel giving the toll charges is still easily readable. A corpse cost nothing, but every living human being had to pay a halfpenny (old money), the same as for a calf, sheep or lamb. And the independent-minded proprietors, being no respecters of persons, went on: 'This bridge being private property every officer or soldier, whether on duty or not, is liable to pay toll for passing over, as well as any baggage waggon, Mail coach or the Royal Family'. In 1934 Queen Mary, the wife of George V, handed over the exact amount during a royal visit. Now there is no charge.

The old iron bridge has a grace and atmosphere all of its own. It seems too fragile to take much punishment, yet it has contended with all that the Severn in spate can throw at it. The first Abraham Darby's grandson, of the same name, had to think out new principles and enlarge his works to make its hundred-foot girders, and experts still argue about where they were cast and how they were transported to the site, with only human and horse muscle available.

Abraham Darby III had been given the job by fellow ironmasters. Preliminary work began in 1777, and the bridge was officially opened on New Year's Day, 1779. Between twenty and thirty men actually erected it, complete with arches and approach roads, and it cost £2,737 4s 4d compared with an estimated £550 (so

The famous iron bridge from which the township took its name

rocketing prices are no new thing!). An extra nine guineas was spent on ale, presumably for the topping-out ceremony.

When the ironmasters decided on their bridge, they were not satisfied with just something that crossed the river. They wanted a township there, providing facilities for their workers and their families. Life could be happier on many modern housing estates if similar thinking applied.

At the north end of the bridge and obviously of the same vintage is a small shopping centre and market house – all handsome Georgian buildings. So is the Tontine Hotel at the west end of the little square, although it has been more obviously done up by its brewery owners. It is only one of Ironbridge's licensed houses – some, such as the Swan a little way upstream, where barges loaded at the Wharfage, are considerably older. But the Tontine, in business three years after the bridge was opened and four years before a similarly named inn downriver at Stourport, was obviously intended to be a feature of the new township.

The hotel's unusual name comes from an Italian banker named Lorenzo Tonti, who thought up a financially profitable way of dicing with death. The share of each subscriber to a capital investment was, at his death, divided among the surviving subscribers until the last of all scooped the pool, which seems a strange principle for Quakers to follow. The Tontine contains two unusual items – the bow window to an inside bar that must once have been on an outside wall, and the splendidly tiled entrance hall. Its tiles were made in the gorge, a little way downstream at the famous Maw works. They must have been considered something special, even by a firm which tiled many hundreds of Victorian churches and hotels, because hidden away is one special tile giving the firm's name, rather like an artist signing a picture of which he is especially proud.

An admirable pamphlet, *Walks in Severn Gorge*, published by the Ironbridge and Coalbrookdale Society and available at the Museum Trust's shops, says of Ironbridge: 'You will have to look hard to find a building less than 100 years old. In fact, from the middle of the bridge you can see just two. The last great change in the town's appearance was the building of the church in 1837'.

Basically Ironbridge is the fossil of a town, as true a fossil as those found abundantly in the gorge's limestone. It was saved before it eroded away and thanks to collaboration between Telford New Town (founded in 1963) and the Museum Trust (set up five years later), it is being preserved for posterity.

Nearly everywhere else, the Industrial Revolution's factories and houses have been demolished and built over, or have fallen down through age. In Severn Gorge, because industry fled to more prosperous sites and there was not enough money about to tackle major improvements, they have remained as frozen as the Sleeping

23

Beauty and her court. Not a beauty in the accepted sense, but then beauty is in the eye of the beholder.

The sites administered by the Museum Trust are worth taking time over. It is no use trying to hurry through them in a day; taking a thorough look at Ironbridge itself takes that. It is becoming a kind of Chelsea in the countryside, with its steep narrow lanes and individually built houses being carefully restored by private owners as well as public bodies.

The steepness of the gorge is breath-taking, in every sense. Gradients greater than one-in-five used to call for extra horses in stage-coach days. To reach Ironbridge Parish Church, by the route the Victorians must have taken, involves a climb up 120 steps from the back of the Tontine. Following sketch maps in the Ironbridge and Coalbrookdale Society's booklet, all except the fit should drive up the narrow streets to St Luke's, near the entrance to which is a sign saying: 'PROHIBITED all vehicles except handcarts, perambulators, invalid carriages and pedal cycles pushed by hand unless requiring access to premises or land adjoining the road'.

The sign is of cast iron, inevitably. So is the one a couple of hundred feet below, on a wall in Wharfside, which says, in a kind of cast-iron shorthand, 'Shrewsby 13 Ironbre Olfur'. Translated, that means thirteen miles to Shrewsbury and one furlong (an eighth of a mile) to the iron bridge itself.

Ironbridge is full of such surprises: in the museum at

Ironbridge School – High Victorian in local brick

24

Abraham Darby's old Coalbrookdale Works, as well as examples of his cooking pots, is a century-old iron pressure-cooker, working on the same principle as modern ones; the abandoned site further up the hill, called The Old Wind, is pronounced with a long 'i' because it was where the winding gear was, at a major canal terminus; at the top of Lincoln Hill, the highest point of the township, pieces of glass are set into a wall to be watched for cracks and if these occur, there has been subsidence; and on a shed beside a cottage at the foot of Coalbrookdale is a plaque marking the height the Severn reached in the Great Flood of 1795, when the river rose twenty feet after a February thaw. The damage was enormous, but the new iron bridge stood the shocks staunchly.

That was because it crosses the river in a single span. In a hard winter the Severn can freeze over, particularly in its upper reaches. With a sudden thaw, chunks of ice perhaps nine inches thick can come hurtling down with sixty miles of gathering momentum behind them. In effect small icebergs, they have demolished bridges at Buildwas and Bridgnorth. But the great engineer Thomas Telford spotted an inherent defect in the design of the iron bridge that the others had missed. They had not allowed for the land on which the bridge's pillars stand moving because the sides of the gorge slip. Now the bridge has more than seventy cracks – but it stands because of remedial work done along lines that he suggested.

St Luke's also has an unusual feature – a purpose-built graveyard. When the church was built, the steps passed along the east end. The Victorians, deciding no church was complete without a burial ground, roofed the steps at the top and built a graveyard that reached up onto it. It gives perhaps the best vantage point of all over the steeply descending roofs and chimneys to the bridge and river – although, another hundred yards uphill from the strangely named old road, Hodge Bower, over Benthall Edge's woods can be seen the white-walled houses of Broseley, at the same height on the other side of the gorge.

A mile downstream is the Museum Trust's biggest showpiece, Blists Hill Open Air Museum, covering more than forty acres and claimed to be the biggest site of its kind in Europe, if not the world. It lies on the north bank and reaching it means passing one of the gorge's two bridges usable by road traffic. This, too, has a distinction. It is Britain's first big reinforced-concrete bridge, built in 1908, six years after one about half its length had been successfully constructed in Lancashire (there was another early small one in Worcestershire, at Stanford-on-Teme). So, as the Ironbridge and Coalbrookdale Society say: 'The Severn Gorge has two unique bridges, each using material which was revolutionary in its time'.

The road to Blists Hill is hummocky and twisty, with warnings about subsidence, and the Ordnance Survey map shows the hillsides above pock-marked by landslips. The entrance up the signposted road is dominated by a huge piece of machinery. The official description is: 'A double-beam blowing engine', and it has the grandiose name of David and Samson. It blew air into blast furnaces to increase the heat (the last time as recently as 1952), on the same principle as a blacksmith's bellows, and it is exceptionally elaborate, with its valves housed in classical columns (cast iron of course). It was built in 1851, the year of the Great Exhibition arranged by Prince Albert, Queen Victoria's husband, so it had to look something special. The massive baulks of timber and the huge iron wheel, with the columns and the elaborate roof, make the mighty machine look rather like a Gréek temple to a god of engineering. There is even the equivalent of a car's piston rings, only on Brobdingnagian scale.

Blists Hill is laid out to show as much as possible of all the kinds of work that went on in this area. The hill itself was mined for coal and clay; iron ore was brought in to feed the blast furnaces, built in the 1830s and 1840s; the canal system which linked industrial Shropshire with the lifeline of the Severn ran through it. So, later, did the railway, derelict long since but still with one end of a bridge in the yard of a pub called the All Nations, which has brewed its own beer for many years.

The buzz of activity at Blists Hill began to die down in 1912, when the blast furnaces closed. The mines were abandoned in 1941, the brick and tile works, using local clays, in the 1950s. Nature took over, so that the Museum Trust even have a booklet about the kinds of weeds and wild flowers that grow on the inhospitable spoil-banks.

Now Blists Hill has life again, but markedly different from that of its heyday. Tourists, youngsters on educational trips, people out for the day – all walk round the places where men, women and children sweated and starved when Britain was the workshop of the world.

Savouring the air and atmosphere at the present Blists Hill is time well spent, because a broad yet intimate picture is presented of how a busy community lived, worked and played at the end of the nineteenth century. The staff wear the costume of the period – all made on the site – with long black skirts, high-necked blouses and shawls for the women, and bracered trousers, wool waistcoats and jackets, mufflers and small caps for the men. Their clogs are also made on the site, because there is a working wood-mill, which turns out the farm gates and timbering of all kinds (even the window frames) used in the site's buildings.

Such Victorian fancies as bull's-eyes, humbugs and toffee apples are sold at the sweet shop from big glass jars. At the candle-makers are sold what were called tallow dips, made on the premises by plunging cotton wicks repeatedly into liquid grease, although now paraffin wax has replaced the foul-smelling mixture of fat from beef and mutton that was called tallow; the candles come in green and the natural yellowish hue because in olden times the green ones were used in the local mines and people caught using them in their homes were thieves.

Other shops at Blists Hill include those of a butcher, a cobbler and a printer, and machinery works spectacularly in a winding-machinery room at the pithead of a clay-mine. Bricks and tiles are made nearby, charcoal produced in a special area, and there is even an old Shropshire toll-house and the stretch of road that was outside it, built when Telford was Shropshire's chief engineer and since lifted from just outside Shrewsbury and brought here.

At the far end of the site, the Hay Inclined Plane solved a major transport problem: how to get raw materials and goods as quickly, simply and cheaply as possible between a plateau and a river two hundred feet below. Two young men won a national competition for their solution, using a modification of a system already working a few miles away. Loaded boats were hauled out of the canal, put in a wheeled cradle and despatched by gravity down rails, each drawing an empty boat up a parallel line as it descended.

The Inclined Plane worked well for more than sixty years until the railways took over and abandoned it. Its last recorded use was in 1894. Undergrowth encroached and hid it until the Museum Trust decided in 1968 that it must be saved, and cleared away the trees and brushwood.

The view from the top is impressive; that from the bottom gives an even better idea of the gradient and of what finally happened to the loads. To reach this vantage point, it is necessary to follow the riverside road downstream to a narrow bridge near the Shakespeare Inn. Steps alongside the village stores provide access to another local phenomenon – a seepage of natural bitumen through the walls of a tunnel running into the Blists Hill slopes. The bitumen used to ooze out into hollows nearby, providing the caulking for the wickerwork coracles that were used in the gorge.

The narrow bridge bestrides a small canal-basin giving access from the Inclined Plane to the Severn and the Coalport China Works. The Tar Tunnel, as it is known, which can be seen only at certain times when guides are available, lies behind a door in the yard of the shop at the roadside.

Everything man-made to be seen sprang from the brain of William Reynolds, described by the Ironbridge Society as 'the man who left more of a mark on the Gorge than any other ironmaster'. His father was managing the Coalbrookdale Works for Abraham Darby III when the girders for the Iron Bridge were cast. William had the idea for Coalport, the canal and river intersection there, the Inclined Plane, wharves and warehouses, factories and cottages for the workers to live in. He even built a successful steamboat and was experimenting with the first steam locomotive when the prototype blew up, killing a workman. That put William Reynolds off; like the Darbys and many other industrial leaders in the gorge, he was a Quaker, with views about the sanctity of human life. He died in 1803, aged 45.

Downriver of the Hay Incline, which did in 3½ minutes what would have otherwise taken three hours using up to twenty-seven locks, bottle-shaped kilns of the Coalport China Works beckon. Here some of the most celebrated chinaware ever produced in Britain originated – including the famous Willow Pattern. The Museum Trust has superb items on view inside the premises, where the buildings are preserved to the minutest detail, even down to the shed occupied by the workman made famous during the television quiz *What's My Line*, the saggermaker's bottom knocker. There is a precise explanation of what he did but basically it was to help produce the rough earthenware cases in which the fine-quality chinaware was baked.

Production-line workshops where the china was made until an amalgamation took the work to Worcester are carefully preserved. One kiln has been segmented like an orange to increase the space for display, and there is also an amazing collection of old documents and newspaper cuttings, including one which brings home why the iron bridge was such a blessing. It recorded a mass tragedy in 1799, when twenty-eight people were drowned and only thirteen saved when the boat in which they were crossing the Severn foundered.

Not much farther on is the last bridge open to the road-user before Bridgnorth. It makes a daunting prospect: wide enough for one vehicle, 10 m.p.h. warning signs, an uneven surface, its handsome cast-iron balustrades strengthened by tubular scaffolding. It makes a fine viewpoint for the half-timbered Woodbridge Inn, well known to fishermen, on what must have been the most toilsome route in the world for many thousands of men down the ages.

Along the south bank, the route which became that of the Bridgnorth-Ironbridge railway until British Rail

The Woodbridge Inn, seen across the rickety bridge furthest downriver in the Severn Gorge

decided in the sixties it was uneconomic, teams of men sweated and strained as they hauled heavy boats against the current, bound for the gorge's mines and industries. And especially for Jackfield, described at the height of the Industrial Revolution as the place with 'the greatest concentration of owners, watermen, bowhauliers (the men who dragged the boats) and horse drivers . . . with many of the characteristics of a port: cheap lodging houses, brothels and numerous public houses'.

The description certainly does not fit present-day Jackfield across-river from Coalport, to which it is linked by a narrow footbridge at the foot of the Inclined Plane. At its centre is something else probably unique to Severn Gorge. The bridge is a war memorial, built after the First World War at the place where a line of trestles had been put up temporarily at each summer's low-water. It is so much more imaginative and useful a tribute than the countless stone crosses or statues of soldiers resting on rifles. A plaque, inevitably of cast iron, obliquely referring to the tolls that used to be charged, says:

The bridge is free, O tread it reverently
In memory of those who died for thee.

The tablet naming those who died in the First World War remembers five or six times as many men as does the nearby one for the Second – a sad reminder of slaughter.

The Boat Inn, at the south end of the Freebridge, as it is called, is the furthest downstream of Jackfield's dwindling number of pubs, and so has always suffered most from the Severn's sudden floods. Crudely cut into the inside of the bar door are lines recording flood levels, the highest of them only a couple of inches from the lintel. A line of tin-tacks, with their heads picked out in white to show up better, spells out '10 FEB 46' – although I think the year of the Great Severn Flood was 1947 and the tacks must have been put in years later.

They still talk locally of the Great Coalport Disaster, referring to the drowning tragedy of 1799, perpetuated in

The spire of Jackfield Church, another example of extravagant Victoriana

29

the newspaper cuttings at the Coalport China Works. They say that the men and women who drowned had their trousers and knickers stuffed with chinaware stolen from their employers, but the thirteen honest ones, un-encumbered, made it to the bank, and from that time on, all workpeople were searched as they left work.

The uneven road between the Boat and the concrete bridge is always slipping and subsiding because it is built on broken tiles, throw-aways from what were probably the two largest tile factories in the world, neighbouring Maw's and Craven Dunhill's. Their products went as far as India (Mysore's famous palace) and Canada (Toronto University). Now an engineering firm uses part of Craven Dunhill's and at Maw's efforts are being made to establish separate industrial units for small firms – including tile-making.

Jackfield Parish Church's most unusual spire is worth more than a casual glance. Sir Arthur Blomfield, its architect in 1863, used bricks of many colours from local clays – reds of all hues, plus yellow and blue. The larger and older church that it was built to augment is now remembered only in the name 'St Mary's Close', used for the municipal houses built on the site where it stood.

CHAPTER TWO

Towards the Beckoning Clees

Broseley leans wearily at the top of the Severn Gorge's steep south slope, like a worn-out workhorse all but drained of life. But in the great coal and iron days, the town was full of fire, in every sense.

Now it is a place of ghosts, notably that of John Wilkinson, who two centuries ago was a figure of fear and admiration at his home next door to Broseley Parish Church. From the east end of the churchyard the Severn can be seen widening after its squeeze through the gorge and flowing surely on below the tree-clad heights of Blists Hill and Sutton Hill until, just beyond Coalport, it swings southwards heading for the Bristol Channel. Also just outside the south door are cast-iron tombstones of which Wilkinson – still a famous name in the iron and steel industry – would have thoroughly approved.

He was perhaps the most adventurous and knowledgeable of all the ironmasters who made the gorge hum (he is the one who is supposed to have first used limestone as a flux when smelting, so avoiding the need to turn coal into coke). Writers of the time say that he could stand on the steps of The Lawns, just north-west of Broseley Church, and look across to the Black Country, where he had smelteries. From the glow in the sky he could tell 'if the iron was coming out properly', and if at all doubtful, he would call for his horse, and no matter what the time or weather, ride the twenty-or-so miles to put things right.

He was certainly the most unprincipled ironmaster. He even exported cannon to the French during the Napoleonic Wars by sending out the barrels as pipes for Paris's new water supply. That nearly resulted in a charge of treason.

But the man who was supposed to think of everything slipped up about the major matter of his own funeral. He decided that cast-iron coffins were the ideal, so he had a couple made, one for himself and the other for anyone he could persuade to buy it. He kept them in his greenhouse and had them brought out at dinner parties so that he could discourse on their virtues.

What happened to the second no-one seems to know, but his own did not bring the fame he expected. When he died, at an estate he had bought in his native Cumbria, his coffin was back in Broseley – and what was more, he had grown too fat for it. They buried him temporarily while they made another, and then the ceremony took place as he had ordained – buried at his own estate, in a cast-iron coffin crowned by a twenty-ton monument, also of cast iron.

But the grave began to subside under the prodigious weight and so he was buried yet again, where rock could support his monument – only for new owners, twenty years later, to decide that they wanted no dead iron-master in their grounds, no matter how famous. So Wilkinson, who even wrote his own epitaph, starting 'Delivered from the Persecution of Malice and Envy, Here Rests . . . Iron Master', was buried for the fourth time, in the graveyard at the chapel of Lindale, near Kendal – separated from his twenty-ton memorial, which stands nearby at the rocky roadside. As a final sad note about the best-laid plans going awry, the Automobile Association's illustrated roadbook, normally so precise, has the entry: 'Lindale. E. C. Thursday. GOLF. An obelisk recalls John Wilkinson, the ironmaster, who modelled an iron bridge in 1786'.

At that cursory dismissal, with the wrong date, Wilkinson should often turn in his iron coffin – although the Broseley legend is that his ghost came back to be seen by the workmen who used to sing a long song about him which ended:

May we always have plenty of stingo and pence,
And Wilkinson's fame live a thousand years hence.

For well over three hundred years Broseley was famous for clay pipes. They smoked 'hot' when using tobacco, but they were also cheap playthings for blowing bubbles, using soapy water, until the 1950s when the present rounded pieces of wire, with detergent, came in. Perhaps that was the death-blow for Broseley's ancient speciality, because no clay pipes have been made in the town since the early 1970s. Three-dimensional pictures (collage work) by local artists often include pipe-bowls collected from spoil heaps as well as tile fragments – not much of an epitaph for an industry that made Broseley nationally famous for its straws, churchwardens and aldermen (the longest stemmed of all the clay pipes). Now complete pipes can be seen only in museums and antique shops, where the bowls have a special collector value. Each had the date and generally the maker's name or initials stamped on it. Later, different shapes and patterns were the identification.

Something should be done to preserve Broseley before it is too late, as the National Trust have done at their nearest stately home to it. This is Benthall Hall, just west on the Much Wenlock road, so historic that it literally illustrates one of the puzzling lines in the old song 'Green

Grow the Rushes O' – the one 'Five for the Symbols at your Door'.

At Benthall the symbols are above the entrance porch on the west side. There used to be five above the south side, too, but during restoration work in 1920 the workmen forgot to put back the top left-hand one, so a plain stone is there instead. The symbols, arranged like a five-card in a pack, represent the five wounds of Christ, the stigmata. To those seeking refuge in times of religious persecution, the symbols meant that aid could be expected within – more a matter of caring for the oppressed than supporting a particular opinion.

Benthall contains the remains of several priests' holes, probably dating back to a major rebuilding in 1583, when Queen Elizabeth I still had twenty years to reign. They are not available to public view, because they are in the private part of the house and Sir Paul Benthall (the word rhymes with 'gentle') still lives there. A link going back to 1120, at the very least, was snapped in 1844 when a clergyman who had married into the family had the hall auctioned – an event recorded with sadness rather than bitterness by Sir Paul (brother of the late Michael Benthall, director of the Royal Shakespeare Theatre) in his personally written notes in the National Trust booklet.

He refers to 'early records being lost' and 'none of the contents of the house have been in it continuously – during the absence abroad of the last owners connected with the original family'. The Benthall who wanted to buy it was a judge in India at the time and could not get back for the auction.

The hall's most notable tenant was Charles Maw, the Jackfield tile-maker, who left his mark on the gardens. He was one of the greatest botanists of his day, with a special interest in the crocus. He travelled widely seeking new species and employing enthusiasts and plant-collectors throughout the world to add to his collection. His *Monograph of the Genus Crocus*, which he personally illustrated, is still of great authority, and there is a superb leather-bound copy in the library at Benthall. Enquiries still come from all parts of the world and in the gardens are many of George Maw's crocuses, which still breed true. There is another reminder of Maw's presence, just inside the churchyard by the most direct walk from the hall – a tiny marble tombstone to a baby daughter.

Benthall Church was rebuilt after the Civil War, in which it was almost razed to the ground during the successful struggle by a Parliamentary garrison to retain possession of the hall, which they had captured to cut off coal supplies to the Royalists at Bridgnorth and Worcester.

The Benthalls recovered their beloved home in 1934, bought back by the granddaughter of the judge. She bestowed it to the National Trust in 1958.

The famous New Forge of ironmaster Wilkinson lay along a lane on the opposite side of the main road from

Benthall Church, scene of a Civil War siege

Benthall's entrance. It is near the Lodge – a name which recalls a hunting lodge in the once-great Shirlett Forest – but what remains of it is just a hollow in the ground. Yet there his workmen made the world's first iron boat, launched successfully on the Severn in front of thousands who came from all around to scoff 'because everybody knows that iron won't float'.

Little remains, either, of the house in Shirlett Forest of a man perhaps even better known among the fashionable set at the turn of the eighteenth century than Wilkinson. He was George Forester, the Squire of Willey, who lived at Willey Old Hall, abandoned for the present New Hall a few years after his death in 1811.

He was the personification of fox-hunting squires, a man of whom it was written: 'Up at four o'clock on a hunting day, he would eat breakfast of under-done beef and eggs beaten up in brandy, after which he was ready for a 50-mile run.'

He had a major asset in his huntsman, who was regarded as the best in Britain – a local boy named Tom Moody, who was the hero of a song which became all the rage in London. But Tom was too fond of drink, which killed him off years before the Squire.

No matter how drunk Tom was, they said, if he was got up in the saddle he would never fall off. His dying wish, as set down by the local writer John Randall, who recorded what happened in Shropshire in those times, was:

I wish to be buried at Barrow under the yew tree in the churchyard and to be carried by six earth-stoppers; my old horse, with my whip, boots, spurs and cap slung on each side of the saddle and the brush of the last fox when I was up at the death at the side of the forelock; and two couples of old hounds to follow me as mourners; when I am laid in the grave, let three halloos be given over me; and then, if I do not lift up my head, you may fairly conclude that Tom Moody is dead.

His wishes were carried out to the letter – but there was no doubt he had gone. As Squire Forester reported in a letter: 'Thus ended the career of poor Tom, who lived and died an honest fellow but alas! a very wet one.'

The Willey estate passed to the Squire's cousin, Cecil Weld Forester, who was also a great fox-hunter and who was raised to the peerage by George IV, a personal friend who was godfather to two of his children, both christened George.

The present Lord Forester is the tenth – the name, according to Randall, goes back to when 'they had been foresters (in charge of a royal forest) in the time of the Henries'.

Apart from special occasions Willey Park is not open to the public, nor is its church, which is used only for services for people on the estate at times like Christmas and Harvest Festival.

The church at Barrow, where Tom Moody is buried, has an Anglo-Saxon chancel and a couple of rusting iron monuments in the churchyard, as well as Tom's stone a few feet from the south door. The old legend that he could not 'sleep easily' still exists among the local people, and children say, 'Tom Moody will get you' if someone misbehaves.

The trail that the Squire and Tom must have followed many times, as foxes streaked for the fastnesses of the Clee Hills looming to the south-west, is more than 'ten honest English miles' – because this countryside carved out of softish red sandstone and marls by swift-running streams would have been heavy going. The steep narrow valleys are havens for wildlife of all kinds, with primroses and violets in the spring and crab apples and hazelnuts in autumn. Fords are as frequent as bridges and there is hardly anywhere large enough to call itself a village. From the number of churches, most with at least a remnant of Norman building, the population must have been much greater than it is now. There are no fewer than six such churches along a six-mile stretch of Brown Clees' eastern slopes, from Ditton Priors in the north to Wheathill in the south, taking in Cleobury North, Burwarton, Aston Botterell and Loughton. And that excludes Neenton, which looks to be Early English but in fact was designed by Blomfield, who also built Jackfield Parish Church.

They exist because of the mineral riches contained in the Clees – coal, iron, limestone and copper, plus the basalt caps which prevented them being eroded away and provide the famous road material called 'dhu-stone'. Now there is nothing economically worth working on the Brown Clees, where quarrying ceased in the mid-1930s.

In all that time, not even a cart-track has been built to the top – women used to carry down the coal on their backs – so the great rolling view is for the walkers. The best approach from the east side is from Burwarton village, which has a Georgian coaching house called the Boyne Arms, after the family owning Burwarton Hall, where royalty have often been guests.

The easiest place to see the effects of coal-mining on the Clees is at a place called The Lubberlands, on Catherton Common, which was remarkable enough to merit an aerial photograph in *English Landscapes* by that great expert Professor W. G. Hoskins. It shows a countryside pitted with craters, almost like a heavily bombed area that vegetation has recaptured. Walk carefully among the bracken and heather and watch out for adders, which like such sunny heathland.

The craters are the remains of medieval pits. What happened was that the miners sank a shaft until they struck coal, then mined out around it until the overhang became dangerous and so was abandoned. The coal was hauled to the surface by windlass and bucket. Abandoned mines collapsed or filled up, leaving a round hollow near the shaft.

The little township of Stottesdon, not far to the east, tells as typical a story, only of what happened on agricultural lands. In Saxon times it was a huge royal manor, with at least eight smaller townships attached that survive as large single farms. Good examples are Pickthorn, whose deserted lanes and houses can still be seen inside a field adjoining the present farmhouse, and Prescott, where a public footpath at the side of farm buildings leads to a two-arched bridge across the River Rea that is supposed to date back to the Romans, whose fort overlooking the Baveney Brook stands at the farm called Wall Town on the B4363 not far south.

In the 1831 Census, Stottesdon was still head of its Hundred, which included thirty-four parishes. Now, although its past importance is indicated by two pubs, it is mentioned in guidebooks only for its church, St Mary's, disproportionately large for the present population of less than a thousand in many times that number of acres. The church has the finest font in Shropshire – a twelfth-century masterpiece of scrolls and designs which look almost as crisp as when they were carved. There is the mystery of the tympanum, the stone which occupies the space between the flat top of a doorway and the arch above it. The Normans delighted in filling this with a carved tablet which generally represents conventional Christian subjects. But not the one at Stottesdon, of which Sir Nikolaus Pevsner comments: 'Possibly of before the Conquest. An emaciated face with a pointed beard is at the top of the arch; at the lintel are three animals caught in a net, two standing on their heads as if

the lintel were meant to be used the other way round, the third standing quite normally.' The church guide suggests that they may be a cat, a dog and a deer.

Shropshire's other famous tympanum is at Aston Eyre, four miles north as the crow flies but more than twice that by the round-about roads. It is of Christ riding into Jerusalem on a donkey on Palm Sunday, and its most unusual feature is that it is partly three-dimensional (you can put your hand in between the front legs).

Tucked away in the lanes to the north-east is Acton Round, where the Norman church was heavily altered in the 1750s – and where the owner of the adjoining manor house has done some remarkable modern alterations to a nearby farm building. Walls of the grey local stone are fronted by concrete mock battlements to imitate a medieval castle because the owner was 'bored with all these tin buildings'.

Morville Hall, on the Broseley/Bridgnorth road is a National Trust property where, to view, an appointment in advance has to be made. At first glance it is entirely Georgian, but it is a rebuilding of an Elizabethan mansion which in its turn was built with materials from the dissolved Benedictine priory which stood on the site back in the twelfth century. About the only trace of the Benedictines' presence is the long oblong of still water at the bottom of the garden that constituted their fish pond. The real impact of the hall is from the outside. Its grey stone walls are topped by gilded domes (the design of

Morville Hall, buildings across the lawn from the Norman church

William Baker, architect of Ludlow's Butter Cross), and across a huge close-mown lawn is a Norman church to complete a picture of rural peace. Nearby is the site of the deserted village of Upton Cressett, which was prosperous until suffering the same blow in the fourteenth century as many other places on the Welsh Marches – although whether it was the Black Death or a general financial depression has still to be established. Upton's assessment of £3 6s 8d in 1291 had been cut to seventeen shillings in 1341 because 'the land lies untilled and the tenants of the same have withdrawn because of penury'.

During Henry VIII's reign it was found that Thomas Cressett (hence the two-word name) had enclosed forty acres of arable land, and later the road running through was stopped and the park enclosed. Of the former village, only a few grass-grown tumps remain around Upton Cressett Hall and gatehouse, and the church (inevitably Norman) is now maintained by the Redundant Churches Fund. The hall is open only on Thursday afternoons in summer, like many other members of the Historic Houses Association. So is the gatehouse which, built about 1540, is some forty years older and a remarkably early brick building for the area. Prince Rupert, King Charles's cavalry commander in the Civil War who seems to have slept in nearly as many places as Queen Elizabeth herself, is reputed to have spent a night at Upton Cressett.

Just outside Bridgnorth is Astley Abbots, famous for its

Redundant now, but Upton Cressett Church remains a credit to its builders

Maiden's Garland. This is inside the church, facing the entrance, and is a heart-shaped wooden framework decorated with gloves, cloth and ribbons of varying colours, with a ribbon-like piece of paper threaded through saying, in handwriting still legible, that it commemorates Hannah Phillips, who died on the eve of her wedding in 1860. Such garlands were the fashion to commemorate maidens who died before marriage. Hannah was drowned crossing the Severn to her

39

Isolated Prescott, one of the widely scattered hamlets in the parish of Stottesdon

wedding, and wreaths of roses, cypress and laurel are still placed under her garland.

Louise Wright, collaborating with the late James Priddey in *Heart of England* in this series, described going by canoe from Bridgnorth to Bewdley. The ways by land use roads running inside Severn's great loop. One passes the entrance to the park which houses Kinlet Hall and the church of St John Baptist.

The hall is no longer a stately home – it has been a boys' prep school since 1940 – but the church is well worth a visit to see its four monumental effigies, all of alabaster. They have been compared with the better-known ones at Tong, north of the Severn on the Staffordshire border. They include one to a man whose ghost had to be exorcized, Sir George Blount, who died in 1584 and who was known as 'The Terror of Scotland'. He became the terror of his own park, too, after his death, because people said they had seen him emerge from the depths of the park's pool mounted on horseback, and ride to his cellars to make sure there had been no pilfering. Clergy, called in with 'bell, book and candle', compelled the apparition to crawl into a bottle, say reports of the time, and this was kept sealed, on his tomb, until it vanished supernaturally – or someone stole it.

In the chancel is a tablet to Captain Charles Baldwyne Childe (the Childes followed the Blounts at Kinlet), who was killed in the Boer War leading an attack on Sugarloaf Hill ('now called Childe's Hill'), and in the churchyard is an even more evocative war memorial. After the First World War, the parishioners restored a medieval cross as a memorial to their dead. It bears nine names, no fewer than four of them Trow. The last of the Trows of Kinlet, the village postmaster for many years, died in 1977.

Another way between Bridgnorth and Bewdley is along the Severn Valley Railway, which since 1970 has chugged along a track between the river and the Wyre Forest. The line, which used to carry on through the Severn Gorge to Ironbridge, was closed by British Rail in 1963, but enthusiasts bought the track before it could be ripped up. They added steam engines and rolling stock and are making a going concern of it, operating a scheduled service throughout the summer.

Mostly single-track, the line sweeps out of Bridgnorth and through rural Hampton Loade to sidings still black with dust at Highley, which was the last surviving pit in this coalfield. It produced about 250,000 tons a year, but was closed by the National Coal Board in 1968 as 'uneconomic', putting 650 men out of work. More recently the little town (also with a Norman church) became notorious for the kidnap and murder, by a man who became known as the Black Panther, of a 17-year-old local heiress.

The train gives intriguing glimpses of the Severn through the undergrowth of hazels, sloe bushes and saplings; there is the nostalgic flavour that steam brings out; and at the stations the paint is fresh, the metalwork

41

The Roman bridge at Prescott, tucked away in narrow lanes

gleaming with polish and elbow grease and the little gardens on the platforms bright with flowers. There are even old enamelled signs, advertising cocoa and whisky, tobacco and matches, at prices ridiculous to modern eyes. At Arley there is even one about soap powder, saying 'the only one in a cardboard packet'.

The line into Bewdley crosses the Severn by the Victoria Bridge, made upriver at Coalbrookdale with a centre-span exactly twice that of the original Iron Bridge, and claimed at the time (1859) to be the largest bridge of its kind in the country.

Nearby is a tunnel used as a setting for a television dramatization of a Charles Dickens short story. The line has also been used for films featuring David Niven and Nicol Williamson. And, with the track recently extended through the local safari park, you can steam, in England, within yards of a pride of lions.

CHAPTER THREE

Land of Cherry Blossom

The road west from Bewdley towards beckoning Titter-stone, the southernmost of the Clees, climbs past the Wood Colliers' Arms, an unusual name for any pub. It commemorates the charcoal burners of the Wyre Forest, which stretches for miles beyond the Forestry Commission's nature-trail centre at Callow Bank and gives rarely explored sanctuary to wildlife of all kinds.

The Dowles Brook – Dowles is a British word meaning 'black' and occurs also as Dawlish in Devon and Dowlais in Wales – provides the easiest access into Wyre for the walker. But for those who want to obtain a whiff of the forest more easily, a minor road runs from Buttonbridge (B4914) across Stirt Common to rejoin the main road west (A4117) at Far Forest – an attractive name for unattractive between-the-wars development. The most striking place on the Stirt Common road is the sharp dip at Furnace Mill, another reminder that iron and coal have been worked here since Roman times. The stone bridge over the Dowles, now enlarged by the Baveney and Mad Brooks, is an ideal place to watch dippers, wagtails and kingfishers as they flit and dive from the trees and shrubs on the banks.

Years before British Rail closed the single-track line that ran through the Wyre Forest, I travelled on it as a boy bound from Ludlow to Bewdley. There was a system of 'rings', I can remember, which had to be exchanged between station-master and driver to make sure the track ahead was clear. And at the little stations there was a great palaver at the loading of the baskets of locally grown fruit – apples, pears, plums and especially cherries. Something in the soil makes this ideal cherry country, and the local growers still pride themselves on the different varieties of reds, blacks and the late-ripening white-hearts. When the blossom breaks, the countryside foams into an overpowering cumulus cloud of creamy-white that is signposted into a 'Blossom Route' about a fortnight after the better-known plum blossom of the Vale of Evesham. Daintier and whiter is the abundant blossom of the gean, or wild cherry, which that famous but morbid poet, A. E. Housman, had in mind when he wrote:

Loveliest of trees, the cherry now
Is hung with bloom along the bough,
And stands about the woodland ride
Wearing white for Eastertide.

Lovely, often-quoted verse – but an example of the fallibility of the author of *A Shropshire Lad*, who wrote his poems more as exercises, exact in technique but lacking local knowledge. After all, one of his few visits to Shropshire was when his ashes were buried at Ludlow. Facts were made to fit, as in the often-derided reference to Hughley steeple, where the church of the village nestling under Wenlock Edge has a tower. This cherry blossom reference also seems to lack local knowledge as Whitsuntide is often cherry blossom time in Shropshire.

Housman wrote, as well, about that unlikely poetic subject, the Wyre Forest railway in one of his longer and, I think, less distinguished poems, which begins:

As through the wild green hills of Wyre
The train ran, changing sky and shire,
And far behind, a fading crest,
Low in the forsaken west
Sank the high-reared head of Clee . . .

The reference to 'changing shire' concerns the boundary between Worcestershire and Shropshire, which follows Dowles Brook, and which the A4117 crosses at the foot of a steep pitch, then runs into Shropshire and on past the Blount Arms. The pub served the old railway station, which was a junction with another defunct line that brought roadstone eleven miles from Ditton Priors' quarries and which had a brief revival during the Second World War because of an enormous ordnance depot in the area. The Blount Arms gave many a man the spirit to reach Cleobury Mortimer, the little town two miles away the station served.

On the way, where the B4204 turns for Clows Top, is the largest tree in Wyre, the Mawley Oak. When measured in 1968, its girth was 23½ feet, and its branches covered more than a quarter of an acre. Just beyond it is Mawley Hall, another home of the Blounts. The station, so it is said, was so far from the town because they insisted that their peace must not be disturbed. The house, open to view by written appointment, has an interior that, says Pevsner, 'was executed obviously without regard to cost and is consequently the finest of its date (1730) in Shropshire'.

Cleobury Mortimer is unmistakable from the moment it comes in sight, because the church's wooden steeple is crooked due to its main timbers warping. It sleeps in the sun now – but that was not so in medieval times. Its name perpetuates that of perhaps the greatest history-makers of all the Marcher lords, the Mortimers. The first, Ralph, fought at the side of William the Conqueror at Hastings, and was rewarded with land where more fighting was needed; keeping back the Welsh, he carved out a small empire. Originally they had three main castles. Henry II appropriated Bridgnorth because the second Mortimer opposed him; Cleobury lost importance as the Mortimers concentrated on their main stronghold at Wigmore; and that in its turn was abandoned for Ludlow.

The site of Cleobury's castle is now covered by a school and houses, with only the old parish church of St Mary, on the slope below to indicate where it was. St Mary's is believed to be the only church in the country with a lay deacon (possibly the survival of a medieval chantry priest); the post is normally offered to the vicar by the Lord Chancellor representing the Crown, because of the royal links with Cleobury through the Mortimers that still exist. Cut off though it is, Cleobury still wears an air of independence, with cobbled sidewalks, a stone block for horse-mounting outside its Elizabethan half-timbered Talbot Hotel and a 1702 brick manor house.

Even more remote, under the south-east slopes of Titterstone, is the hamlet of Hopton Wafers, where one of the biggest of the hurrying streams, the Mill Brook caused local postman-poet Simon Evans to write:

Were you ever at Hopton's Crown
Where the road goes up and the brook goes down?

He might not have been in Housman's class, but he knew his countryside intimately and lovingly, although he was a 'furriner' from Liverpool. He was written off as a 'hopeless case' after being wounded and gassed in the First World War, but after eight years in convalescent homes cajoled the Post Office into giving him the kind of job that exists no more. He was appointed the postman for the scattered farms and isolated hamlets of a nine-mile stretch along the River Rea. Every day he walked its course from Cleobury Mortimer to a little shelter just east of Stottesdon, delivering the mail. Then he walked back, blowing a whistle to tell people he was there to collect their letters and parcels. With a shattered body and ruptured lungs, he did not breathe easily, but when, as a young reporter, I met him, his eyes lit up as he quoted George Borrow's *Lavengro*.

He wrote a couplet that smacks of Gypsy Petulengro:

The sun, the stars, the wind, the rain
Gave me back my life again.

I may have misquoted, because I have not read his *Around the Crooked Steeple* for years, and it is out of print. But his courage and the sunshine he gave to so many people extended his life until 1940, when he stayed on in the countryside he had grown to love by having his ashes scattered on top of the Brown Clee. He would have appreciated one sign among the bric-à-brac in the Crown's medieval dining room: 'Take notice that as from this date poachers shall be shot on sight and if practicable questioned afterwards.' It is dated November 1, 1868, and the wording is supposed to come from a local estate.

The brook hurries down to join the Rea at Neen Sollars, one of three hamlets containing the river's old name, the Neen (which is presumably why the pronunciation is 'Ree' and not 'Ray'). The others are Neenton, where it rises, and Neen Savage, on the other side of Cleobury and notable for its ford; there is a nine-foot flood-marker and on the footbridge alongside, at least six feet higher, a sign saying it marks the height of the flood on September 26, 1946. Neen Sollars has expensively restored black-and-white houses and, in the thirteenth-century church, an alabaster monument to Humfrey Conyngsby, who lies gazing at the ceiling, his head propped on his right hand, as if trying to remember for

The ford at Neen Savage, cut deep in the soft red marl

Although the railway vanished long ago from Neen Sollars, its presence is perpetuated

ever the four famous travels he undertook between 1594 and 1610, when he vanished in Venice, never to be heard of again. He was the Lord of the Manor and his sister had the monument erected according to instructions he had left, realizing the dangers of travel in those times.

The south-eastern slopes of Titterstone Clee seem to roll endlessly upwards from the vantage-point of the quaintly named Live and Let Live Inn. Coal was dug on that high common land well before Tudor times – and even now around here cornfields, meadows and orchards are under recurring threats from opencast mining. In this miniature Forest of Dean small pits were worked until after the Second World War producing coal rich in sulphur which was supposed to give the Teme Valley hops a better flavour and in the mid-1970s a pit was sold to two businessmen that was estimated to have a million tons of good coal still available. At Mamble, the largest village in the coalfield, is the Sun and Slipper which doubly commemorates the Blounts. The Sun was their emblem, the Slipper recalls a supposed medieval raid when one of the family, staying at the inn, fought off the attackers and lost a slipper in the process.

Mamble Church is nearly eight hundred years old and nearby Bayton has a Norman font, but probably the most interesting church is that at Rock. The parish church here (the name 'Rock' is derived from 'oak' and not the stony 'rock') escaped the restorations of Victorian enthusiasts that have made Worcestershire so barren for medieval 'church collectors' and is full of amazing Norman carving. Some of the figures seem to have no Christian significance, such as a woodwose, the mythical wild man of the woods. In the church, too, are the village's stocks and whipping post.

Totally different is the church at Great Witley, half-way on towards the Severn, which dates back to the days of George II, and is regarded as Britain's finest baroque church (the only possible challenger is in Middlesex). It stands alongside a pot-holed lane, with a plain exterior that has been unkindly compared with a warehouse. Inside is a great glow of colour emphasized by the white walls with their gilded motifs – a Venetian chapel in the heart of rural Worcestershire. What happened was that a Midland industrialist named Foley bought a Jacobean house, rebuilt it more grandly, and planned his own church in the grounds. He died three years before it was opened and his widow had him remembered by a gigantic monument, nearly as large as the one at Blenheim to the Duke of Marlborough.

It clashes with everything else in the church, because twelve years after the official consecration, the first Lord Foley's son bought the chapel that the first Lord Chandos had built at Edgware – part of the great mansion the spendthrift heir was selling off. The ecclesiastical jewel – elaborate ceilings, bright pictures, gilded ornaments, painted glass – was transported to Great Witley and made to fit the church. This is betrayed by two 'not quite

Great Witley Church, baroque inside its plain exterior; the thick coursing of the wall indicates the steepness of the climb

right' panels in the ceiling above the organ case, which once held an instrument that Handel played.

The first Earl of Dudley, a Foley descendant, converted Witley Court into a house so princely that Edward VII became a frequent visitor. Then, one fateful night in 1937, much of the semi-palace was destroyed by fire. Plans to auction it failed because the sale date coincided with the 1938 Munich Crisis. The great house is a crumbling wreck with County Council 'Danger, Keep Out' warnings. In the grounds are the remains of two massive fountains; the larger one, the Perseus Fountain, has as its centrepiece a prancing horse which would stand twenty-six feet above water-level – if there was any water there! The church, even more desperate than most for money because of the effects of dampness on its paintings, has a fascinating fund-raising collection of old photographs, newspaper cuttings and so on. Most refer to Witley Court's days of glory, such as one caption that says: 'Famous pioneer of aviation Gustave Hamel stands by his plane at the Court, having carried Lady Dudley as a passenger from Worcester on 26th February, 1914. She afterwards went up with him again and they looped the loop over the Court'.

West of Witley loom the heavily wooded Abberley Hills, also threatened by quarrying (although for limestone in their case). The highest is Woodbury, topped by a large British camp; the Abberleys have been used strategically down the centuries because of their position

Great Witley Court – detail of statue at the centre of the Great Fountain

overlooking the Teme and its junction with the Severn. It may well have been here, for instance, that the famous meeting between St Augustine and the Celtic bishops took place in A.D. 602 as chronicled by the Venerable Bede. Other claimants range from Cressage, Shropshire ('Christ's Oak') to Aust, Gloucestershire (abbreviation of 'Augustine'). But the Rev. J. Louis Moillet, Rector of Abberley 1865-1904, after years of research, confidently claimed that the oak under which the historic meeting took place stood near the lodge-gate to the present Abberley Hall. He wrote that the oak, so old that it was hollow, was thatched to serve as a turnpike house, but

one night in the early nineteenth century its keeper set it on fire accidentally and it was destroyed.

Abberley is locally famous for the clock-tower in the hall's grounds which dominates the countryside for miles around. It was built in Victorian times by a family called Jones who had prospered 'in trade'. Reputedly their reason was so that they could literally look down on Witley Court which, metaphorically speaking, looked down on them. There is also a famous restaurant at The Elms, once the home of one of Nelson's officers, Admiral Maling.

The old village of Abberley is tucked away north of Abberley Hill. In it, unexpectedly grand seventeenth- and eighteenth-century houses face the old Manor Arms. The pub's sign has a link with the Norman Conquest, as it includes the arms of Raoul du Todeni. He was the hereditary standard-bearer of Normandy who was granted Abberley after carrying William's dedicated banner at Hastings. But Abberley's gem is what remains of the church that the du Todenis built and which the Victorians discarded because it was 'decayed and damp'. Little more than the chancel is left, with a notice saying: 'A Norman church on Saxon foundations' – but housed within is John Blamyre's bell. It is believed to be one of only seven of its time surviving, all the others being in the North Country. He was a Cumbrian abbot, a man who lived so blameless a life that at the Dissolution of the Monasteries, it is recorded, 'even Henry VIII felt he had

The little Norman church at Abberley, built on a Saxon site

to do something about it so made him Rector of Abberley in recompense'. He was even allowed to bring 'his beloved bell', used in the Roman Catholic Church's 'Ave' (the 'Hail Mary'). It escaped being melted down in later persecutions because it did not bear the word 'Maria' and in 1874 it had another narrow escape when it was not sold with the church's other bells because it was cracked.

The most spectacular way out of the village is by Winniatts Way which climbs steeply over Abberley Hill from a few yards south of the old church, giving glimpses to the north of the Wyre Forest, brooding beyond the hilly farms which were wrested from it and which are noted for their fruit, particularly plums, damsons and cherries.

The highest of the Abberley Hills is Woodbury – the furthest point into England ever reached by an invading French army. Joining Owen Glendower and his Welshmen in the 1402 revolt, they camped on top of Woodbury with the English King and his army glowering at them from Abberley Hill. The more daring spirits duelled with each other in single-combat on the flat land where the Hundred House Hotel now stands. As an old historian writes: 'They had a fine slope on each side to rush down to the duel.' But the invading army had at last to draw back when supplies ran out, losing many stragglers in the flooded Teme.

Woodbury's last historic moment occurred during the Civil War, when the ordinary people turned against the depredations of both sides, in what became known as the Clubmen's Revolt. In March 1645, some two thousand people, meeting on the hill, passed a resolution for 'all the inhabitants of north-west Worcestershire' saying: 'We, our wives and children, having been exposed to utter ruin by the outrages and violence of the soldiers, are now forced to associate ourselves in a mutual league for each other's defence – against all murders, rapines, plunder, robberies or violence which shall be offered by the soldier or any oppressor whatsoever.' To show they meant it, they bought guns, ammunition and other arms.

Now 'utter ruin' seems far away from the rich farming hamlets that pair off in this fertile stretch of the Teme Valley, where the soil matches the coats of the plump Hereford cattle munching lush pasture in fields bordered by damson trees and hedgerows over which wild hops climb. A typical couple of these small huddles of farm-houses and cottages are the Shelsleys – Shelsley Beauchamp bearing the family name of the later famous Earls of Warwick, and Shelsley Walsh – the Walshes supplying Henry VIII with a Chancellor of the Exchequer. The former, on the north bank, has a church of the same rich colour that the plough turns up in the fertile fields that border it. The latter is on an escarpment so steep that since 1904 it has staged the world's oldest motor hill-climb. Shelsley Walsh's church takes some finding – the best thing to do is to make some local enquiries – which is presumably why it is one of the few churches in Britain retaining its medieval rood beam, the spar of timber where chancel and nave join which bore the cross of Christ (called the 'rood') before the Reformation. Above it remains the crudely painted roof of blue dotted with golden stars, signifying Heaven.

The church is built of a softish limestone called tufa, quarried from the Southstone Rock protruding from the escarpment about a mile upriver. A few thousand years ago a petrifying stream deposited its dissolved limestone in what is in effect a stalagmite fifty feet high. The Normans used a lot of tufa (its more high-sounding name is travertine) because it is easy to quarry; weathering, though, makes it as full of holes as a Gruyère cheese. At Eastham Church, four miles upstream, the pinkish-grey of tufa is emphasized by the red-brick tower added in 1835.

Another pair of twin villages are Stockton-on-Teme and Stanford-on-Teme, linked by Stanford Bridge – near which took place one of the earliest motor-car double fatalities on record. At the bottom of a steep hill on the road from Great Witley is a cast-iron plate on a post in front of an oak, saying: 'MOTOR ACCIDENT Shelsley 19th Jan 1906. Planted as a landmark and as a protection to travellers.' What happened was that a car carrying supporters of the father of Stanley Baldwin (who became Prime Minister and later Earl of Bewdley) crashed into an orchard when its brakes failed, as it returned from Great Witley polling station at the 1906 General Election. Two men died later from their injuries.

Stanford Church, rebuilt in the reign of George III, has an alabaster monument going back to the fifteenth century. St Andrew's at Stockton, where an aged hop-bine clambers over the porch, has one two centuries older, with a long tombstone to its first rector in Latin that translates as: 'Given as a prey to death there lies here Redelphus . . . in great peace'. Also inside is a monument in wood, with remarkably few worm holes, to one of the Walshes, similar to another back at Shelsley Walsh. But life as it was locally, before modern hustle and bustle, is best summed up by four identical crosses side by side to the west of the church. They commemorate the Atthills who lived at Aniceford, the big house on the hill towards Abberley. Martha, the mother, a clergyman's widow, died in 1910, aged 89. Her three maiden daughters (there were also three other children) lie beside her – Alice, who died in 1942, aged 91; Emily, died 1929, aged 83; and Florence, died 1936, also aged 89. While they lived in the village they shared in its life, and are still remembered.

The reddest church of all is at Martley, where a blue-grey lichen that flourishes on the sandstone covers so much of the tower that it could almost have been unskilfully daubed with paint (there is something of the same effect back at Shelsley Beauchamp). It is a church full of treasures, notably medieval wall paintings that escaped

Clipped yew cross in the churchyard at Martley

Also in the loop are Holt, Lower Broadheath where, lovingly preserved, is the 'cottage birthplace' of Sir Edward Elgar, the famous composer. It has been maintained by the Elgar Foundation since 1936, two years after his death, when Worcester Corporation bought it because its future was threatened. The signposting is modest, but the visit is well worth while – to see such personal trivia as Elgar's golfclubs and his wind-up gramophone, as well as the manuscript score of his Second Symphony.

the restorers. In the churchyard is a huge clipped yew cross. It must be eighteen feet high and twelve feet across, with shaft and arms approaching six feet square. One man started it at about the turn of the nineteenth century, and his descendants still clip it.

The Teme suddenly swings below Martley, through the gap between Ankerdine Hill and the northern foot-hills of the Malverns. Enclosed in its great loop is Astley, which has a Norman church abounding in interesting monuments, a mill with an abnormally high weir and Astley Hall, where Earl Baldwin died.

Astley's picturesque mill-house

Holt Castle, now a private residence

CHAPTER FOUR

Forever Faithful City

The Teme merges with the Severn in fields green and luxuriant almost beyond imagination, sliding in so imperceptibly that Elgar is credited with saying he wished to be buried here. But appearances can be deceptive, and not only because floodwaters often cover the land. For this is Powick, a place that twice saw hard fighting in the seventeenth-century struggle between King and Parliament: the opening clash that gave the Royalist cavalry an enduring moral advantage, and the final tactical stroke that gave Oliver Cromwell his 'crowning mercy' and set Charles II off on his long flight that ended in France by way of an oak tree in Shropshire and a disguise as a country yokel.

The historic bridge at Powick, where the Civil War fighting began, is a key point to a triangle of three decisive battles in English history – to follow this will mean visiting Worcester, with its present-day population of seventy thousand; peering into the Vale of Evesham as far as its main town; and then ambling along the final twisting miles of Shakespeare's Avon before it joins the Severn at Tewkesbury.

Altogether, it is a triangle full of England's riches, where much of the nation's history was made. The battles arranged in date order are: Evesham, where Henry III's son Edward (who became Edward I seven years later) ended the Barons' War in 1265 by defeating Simon de Montfort; Tewkesbury, where the Yorkist Edward IV put the Lancastrians out of the Wars of the Roses in 1471, executing the leaders who escaped slaughter on the battlefield; and Worcester, where in 1651 Cromwell stormed the defences and scattered Charles II's army to the four winds.

Powick's historic bridge is not the single-span iron arch which carries the road from Great Malvern into Worcester, but a narrow brick and stone one a hundred yards upstream, approached along a pot-holed lane. The Teme runs deep between steep banks here with no fewer than three flood-markers, climbing above each other. And from the bridge, just about wide enough for two cavalry horses abreast, it is easily apparent what happened on that September day in 1642.

A troop of Parliamentary horsemen trotted over it, aiming to outflank King Charles I's bullion train heading north. When they were just over the bridge they bumped into a crack Royalist cavalry force, resting in a field after a hot and tiring ride south on a similar outflanking movement. The Cavaliers, commanded by the famous Prince Rupert, reacted more quickly and had ground in which to form up. They hurled their opponents back into the Teme and cut them down. At least fifty of the Parliamentary men were killed, a dreadful casualty rate for such small forces. The little road became known as Cut Throat Lane, but it no longer exists. It has been overgrown by a modern housing estate, with every Way, Drive or Close named after a place in Canada and not a Civil War reference in sight.

The Teme at Powick again ran red with blood nine years to the day later. The main forces of Charles II (still mourning his father's execution two years before) were at the Sidbury Gate, Worcester, on the road in from London, and his rear must have seemed secure, with just one bridge across the Severn and the Teme in her lower reaches giving added protection. Charles had surveyed the entire scene that very morning from the tower of Worcester Cathedral, nearly two miles upriver from Powick, and must have been satisfied, particularly with good-quality Scottish troops defending the line of both rivers. But the master tactician Cromwell saw a weakness and exploited it.

He hurried extra men to Powick, had temporary bridges built across both rivers, caught the 'back-door' defenders in the rear and rushed back to the main action, across land now occupied by Cherry Orchard and other housing estates. He was out to deal with Charles's main strength, manning an earthworks called Fort Royal, just outside the Sidbury Gate, while his men at Powick destroyed the retreating Royalists who were stumbling back to Worcester Bridge across the water-meadows which now accommodate sports grounds, including Worcestershire County Cricket Club's famous pitch. Few made it to the bridge, which was succeeded by the present much more sumptuous affair, built 1771–80 and since enlarged. The two earlier stone bridges were slightly upstream.

Worcester's information centre is at the Guildhall – which bears its own reference to the Civil War. The city itself is best explored on foot because of the traffic problems, nine 'A' roads descending on the bridge. Piecemeal demolition has left the city rather like a huge jackdaw's nest, with treasures glittering in unexpected spots. The information centre solves that problem with an admirable pamphlet giving a route that covers the high spots by foot in less than two hours and which can be shortened. The Guildhall is in High Street, Worcester's main traffic artery until new roads bypassed a central section early in 1980. It provides a good example of why Worcester can be difficult for the stranger, because in three miles it has ten different names: Barbourne Road (at the north end), Upper Tything, The Tything, Foregate Street, The Cross, High Street, College Street (where the cathedral is), Sidbury, London Road, and Red Hill. Fortunately the Guildhall, between the cathedral and an obvious railway bridge over the main street, is unmistakable. An impressive brick and stone façade is crowned by an enormous carved central pediment, the whole dating back to 1721–3. It is attributed to Thomas White, a Worcester man who was a pupil of Sir Christopher Wren.

Although the Civil War had been over for seventy years when the Guildhall was built, the feelings of hatred in Worcester were perpetuated. Cromwell's likeness is nailed by the ears above the main entrance, with Charles I and Charles II posed elegantly at full length in niches left and right of him. Above all a statue of Queen Anne gazes down plumply and somewhat patronizingly.

Inside the Guildhall is a sumptuous assembly room with one of the most ornate ceilings to be found anywhere in the area. On one of the walls, among a mass of paintings of celebrities, is a full-length portrait of George III, presented by that monarch after a visit in 1788. The assembly room, and further rooms in the building containing armour and other interesting items, are open to the public at times the information centre can supply.

Although the cathedral seems the obvious place at which to start a tour of Worcester, in many ways it is more convenient first to seek out some of the few historic half-timbered buildings that remain in the city. There was such a mighty pulling-down and redevelopment in the 1960s, in the name of progress for traffic-routing and shopping services, that Worcester looks less like an ancient cathedral city than any of those with which it should compare, such as York and Chester.

Take, for instance, the famous house from which Charles II made his escape after his main strongpoint at Sidbury Gate had been overrun and it was obvious all was lost. It stands where the corn market is joined by New Street, up which he must have galloped his charger. The house is best approached by St Swithun's Street (on the opposite side of High Street from the Guildhall) and the wonderfully named Mealcheapen Street. Charles beat one of Cromwell's officers to it by a short head and nipped out of the back, over the city walls and away. It is a romantic story – but now in an unromantic setting, a redeveloped shopping area. The half-timbered building is smaller than expected, because much of it was destroyed by fire at the end of the eighteenth century. In recent years it has become a shop and the famous inscription cut into a main outside beam, 'Love God, honor ye King' (note the American-style spelling) and the date 1577, when the house was built, is painted in the same black as the rest of the woodwork, so as to be hardly readable. Worst of all when the dual-carriageway bypass road was cut across the back, the blocks of stone that remained of the old town walls over which the King escaped, were taken away.

The ancient New Street runs into the equally old Friar Street, graced by what is perhaps Worcester's finest half-timbered building, 'Greyfriars'. It was probably the last building that the Franciscans (who wore grey habits, hence the nickname) built in Worcester before the Dissolution of the Monasteries, and it passed to Worcester Corporation. Then it was leased to wealthy families, but it gradually lost status until by the beginning of this century it was little more than a multi-occupied slum.

The Worcestershire Archaeological Society found a member to buy it, and decay was just about kept at bay . . . until Mr and Miss Matley Moore, the only brother and sister fellows of the Society of Antiquaries, came on the scene. They made 'Greyfriars' their home, spent many years having it restored and repaired, and finally produced a phoenix from the decay.

'Greyfriars' now dominates Friar Street, with neighbouring half-timbered property acquired and taken into a general setting of a rich house, beautifully furnished and equipped with antique pieces and with a small, Tudor-style garden, with neighbouring buildings matching into the style of living of four centuries ago, including shops. The Matley Moores bestowed the property on the National Trust in 1966 and it is open to

Greyfriars, one of the National Trust's prized possessions in Worcester

59

Worcester – Friar Street, up which Charles II escaped, and which escaped the redevelopers

the public on the first Wednesday afternoon of each of the summer months.

Beyond Friar Street and on the other side of the Worcester-Birmingham Canal is the National Trust's other famous property in the city, the Commandery, marked by a brass plate on the door so polished down the years as to be hardly legible. But its age is nothing compared to that of the building it marks. This was built in the fifteenth century on the site of a hospital (which as well as caring for the sick, aided the poor and sheltered travellers) founded in 1085 by St Wulfstan, Worcester's bishop at the time of the Norman Conquest.

It has the original great hall, with a lofty open roof, and a rich Elizabethan staircase leading to upper rooms, one of which retains sixteenth-century wall paintings. Another feature of the ground floor is an oriel window with original patterned fifteenth-century glass. The Commandery has a special place in history as the headquarters, for the Battle of Worcester, of the King's army – and inside its walls the commander-in-chief, the second Duke of Hamilton, died from his wounds. His descendant, the fifteenth Duke, attended the official opening in 1977 of the Commandery as a tourist centre and museum by Worcester City Council, who sold other property to raise the £385,000 to buy it and fit it out.

This highly commendable step of salvaging something from the post-Second World War despoilment of the Faithful City – even worse than what happened after the Civil War, which cost Worcester the then astronomical sum of £100,000 for the property and £80,000 for citizens' money and goods – was emulated the following year when Worcester Civic Society had city council aid in buying the keyhole-shaped chapel of the Calvinistic Methodist sect known as the Countess of Huntingdon's Connection. Selina, a formidable female of whom one of the Georges is reputed to have said that 'she should have been a bishop', was a widowed countess who established the sect in the mid eighteenth century, and the Worcester chapel built between 1773 and 1815 had an active congregation until the mid-1970s. The almost overpowering interior is notable for the high pulpit flanked by two enormous eagle lecterns and row upon row of the original box pews.

It is just off Deansway, in what is left of what was a human rookery. The best thing to do is to aim for the most notable church spire in Worcester. It is all that remains of the demolished St Andrew's Church, and is known as the Glover's Needle (glove-making being a traditional Worcester trade). At its pinnacle the spire is 245 feet in the air, and its diameter narrows from twenty feet at the base to just under seven inches.

Other city-centre churches well worth visiting – details of their location are best obtained from the information centre – include the city's 'mother church', St Helen's, now the Diocesan Record Office; St Swithun's, notable for its huge three-decker pulpit; and St John's-in-

61

The towering Glover's Needle, the tallest and narrowest spire in Worcester

Bredwardine, back across the river bridge, with much medieval architecture. Then there is the Congregational church just west of Foregate, once described as 'a jolly medley . . . like a tiny and exuberant opera house', and the Roman Catholic church in Sansome Place where Elgar succeeded his father as organist.

There remains Worcester Cathedral and its precincts. The information service available inside and the helpfulness of the well-read guides make great depth of detail superfluous in a book of this length. The treasures range from St Wulfstan's crypt, its massive strength dating back to the saint's rebuilding started in 1084, to the view from the top of the tower. Norman architecture abounds but even more impressive is the choir and Lady Chapel, built in the Early English style over more than a century from 1224 onwards. It is almost like a church within a church, with a high vaulted roof supported on a forest of slender polished pillars which look almost black and are in fact of Purbeck marble – which is not a true marble but a limestone abounding in the shells of fresh-water snails quarried in the Isle of Purbeck, Dorset, and exported to Europe as well as sent to top-class building sites throughout England.

It is probably the nearest approach to marble to be found in Britain, and is very hard, as the effigy of King John instances. This dates back to a few years after his death in 1216, yet looks almost as good as new except for a slightly damaged nose. There he lies, with head looking

Worcester Cathedral from the riverside

east . . . the first of the Angevin kings not to be taken back to France for burial. In his will, which still exists, John stipulated he was to be buried at Worcester and his body was brought from Newark, where he died of dysentery after that disastrous affair in The Wash of which all schoolchildren know. The effigy is, in fact, the lid of his original stone coffin, opened in 1797, and it now rests on a sixteenth-century tomb chest.

The other royal interment in the cathedral is that of Prince Arthur, the elder son of Henry VII. His death at the age of 16, soon after his marriage to Catherine of Aragon, left the way clear for his younger brother, Henry VIII, to succeed to the throne, marry the young widow as the first of his six wives, and change Christian history.

Arthur died at Ludlow (dealt with in a later chapter) in April 1502, and his sumptuous cortège travelled through the Wyre Forest – a contemporary wrote, 'It was the foulest cold windye and rainey daye, and the worst way, that I have ever seen' – to Bewdley and then down Severnside, staging overnight at various churches, to Worcester. Two years later building began of the chantry chapel that surrounds the prince's simple tomb. The stonework is so sumptuous that it is believed that Henry VII sent his best masons from Windsor to construct it.

The cathedral overflows with riches and memorials, from bishops' tombs to the small slab near the west door marking the ashes of Stanley Baldwin, Prime Minister during Edward VIII's abdication, and from the tablet in the north transept commemorating author Francis Brett Young, brought back from South Africa for burial in his beloved Worcestershire, to the obscure stone in the cloisters that bears just the word 'Miserrimus'. That means 'the most miserable of men' and when Wordsworth once saw it he wrote a poem about what a misspent life a man with such a memorial must have led – whereas in reality Thomas Morris, who was deprived of his living as vicar of nearby Claines because he remained loyal to the Stuarts, lived in poverty and hope for nearly fifty years and died at 88 soon after the Young Pretender's defeat at Culloden convinced at last that the Stuart cause was lost.

From the cathedral a Norman doorway leads into College Green, which gives the best impression of what Worcester looked like in monastic times, and is also a haven of peace away from the traffic roar a couple of hundred yards away. At the bottom of the slope, through ornamental gardens to the river side, is the Watergate, the way by ferry into Worcester when the city was walled. On the Watergate's walls are inscriptions recording the heights reached by record floods. Topmost of all, a tablet recording the floods of 1672 and 1770, is about an inch above the record for recent years set up in 1947.

Back in College Green, the houses are all unalike but blend together as a typical cathedral close. One of them, identifiable through his writings, is that visited by the diarist Francis Kilvert for the funeral of his aunt,

View from Worcester Cathedral grounds

described so acutely as to make humorous reading of what seems an impossible subject. And on the east side is the remnant of one wall of what was the monastery's Guesten Hall, built about 1320 and demolished in 1859. It had a huge oak roof which Sir Nikolaus Pevsner describes as 'the most elegant of medieval carpentry in Worcestershire'. The roof was saved by being slightly altered and used as the roof of Holy Trinity, built in Worcester's Shrub Hill area in 1863, but this in its turn was demolished in the early 1970s. Fortunately the Guesten Hall roof was again preserved, although to see it now you have to go to the Avoncroft Museum of Buildings just south of Bromsgrove.

Perhaps Worcester is more unfortunate than most cities and towns in the fate of its old buildings, it does seem to have suffered a lot. Even the Guildhall was once threatened – and there was the case of the lych gate, the only one for a cathedral in the country. The Ministry of Works sent a team to preserve it, but rather in Mother Hubbard style, when they got there the cupboard was bare. The lych gate had already been demolished to make way for a new shopping precinct!

The way out of College Green is through the Edgar Tower, restored externally by the Victorians, but essentially the remaining tower of Worcester Castle. The famous Royal Worcester porcelain works are to the right – these were established in 1751, and conducted tours are available. Adjacent is the Dyson Perrins Museum, which

The cathedral close at Worcester

is open all the year round except Sundays (and some Saturdays in winter). It contains the most comprehensive collection in existence of the firm's products down more than two centuries.

The road from Worcester to the Vale of Evesham crosses the M5 just before Spetchley Park where Cromwell slept before the Battle of Worcester, although in the predecessor of the present house, which was built north of the old one, about the time of the end of the Napoleonic Wars. The house is not open to the public, but thirty acres of gardens are, with a splendid collection of trees and shrubs which are particularly attractive in late spring. Both red and fallow deer roam the park, and ornamental wildfowl are on the lake on which the house fronts.

The church on the other side of the road is worth looking at, too. Spetchley is the home of the Berkeleys who also own the famous Berkeley Castle in Gloucestershire, and there are family memorials and a Berkeley Chapel in the church.

At the next crossroads the B4804 drops down to Evesham along the Avon's north bank. On the left are the villages that make a day's excursion on their own – with the essential aid of an Ordnance Survey map, to negotiate the intricate maze of lanes through rich farming country and half-timbered brick and stone villages. Each has its own touch of individuality, although differences would have been greater before Victorian restorers,

backed by the opulence of the age, got to work on the medieval heritage.

Broughton Hackett has an exceptionally large seventeenth-century water mill, Upton Snodsbury a Perpendicular tower on St Kenelm's, Grafton Flyford its church paintings on square boards going back to Elizabethan times at least, Flyford Flavell two pleasant Jacobean benches in St Peter's, Naunton Beauchamp the impressive half-timbered Naunton Court. Then the scattered hamlet that bears that most rounded title, White Ladies Aston – so named because until the Dissolution of the Monasteries it belonged to Cistercian nuns at Worcester, who wore white habits. In the church is a memorial to a vicar who held the living for seventy-one years before he died at 99. Then there is Peopleton, where a beam carved with a delicate leaf frieze is part of the former rood screen; Pinvin, an obscure-looking village with church wall paintings, whose name has been claimed to come from 'Penda's Fen', Penda being the pagan king of the Mercians in the seventh century; and Throckmorton, perched more than 120 feet above the Avon, where a timber-framed medieval house, Court Farm, was the home of the Throckmortons (whose name is perpetuated in the City of London's Throgmorton Street) before they moved just over the Warwickshire border to Coughton Court, near Alcester.

Throckmortons are commemorated in the Norman church at Fladbury in the valley below, where the Avon has formed a great loop in the struggle to find gradients in such flat land. Silt deposited by floods contributes to making this some of the most fertile land even in the Vale of Evesham, and archaeological finds prove that men have lived here since the Early Bronze Age, something like three thousand years ago. There was a monastery at Fladbury as early as 691, in which year the then King of Mercia gave land to the second Bishop of Worcester, Oftfor, to have it converted into an abbey, but this was never done because in 702 the next Bishop of Worcester, St Egwin, decided to found one at Evesham instead.

Fladbury has handsome houses, a bridge over the Avon, a mill (now a private house) that is mentioned in Domesday Book as having an annual rental of five hundred eels, and the second deepest lock in the Lower Avon Navigation between Tewkesbury and Stratford.

The church's chief treasure is a Virgin and Child panel of fourteenth-century glass that has been exhibited at the Louvre in Paris and the Victoria and Albert Museum in London; it is now the centrepiece of an oak cross behind the Lady Chapel altar. Nearly as celebrated are six windows dating from the following century, believed to have been brought from Evesham Abbey at the Dissolution and depicting the arms of Simon de Montfort and other knights who fought at the Battle of Evesham, three miles eastwards.

CHAPTER FIVE

The Fertile Vale of Avon

It was in 1265 that the battle took place that put Evesham's name in the history books. But the settlement inside a major Avon loop dates back to more than 560 years before.

That was when Egwin, the third Bishop of Worcester, filched the fame that might have been Fladbury's by setting up a Benedictine community where a swineherd named Eoves, employed by the bishop, said he had seen a vision of the Virgin Mary.

Egwin, a man of great faith or business acumen (charitably, both) went to the very spot, reported seeing the same vision and founded what became one of the wealthiest and most powerful abbeys in the land. He became the first abbot and was later canonized, which brought pilgrims flocking to Evesham Abbey.

Abbots good and abbots bad came and went, notably one appointed by John when acting as regent for his brother, Richard the Lionheart. Some suggested that the appointment was to spite the then Archbishop of Canterbury, because Roger Norreys, the new abbot,

according to a monkish chronicler, was: 'Puffed up, pompous in his speech, treacherous in his actions, covetous in his preferences, a despiser of religion, cringing to his superiors, contemptuous to his inferiors, gaudy in his clothing, negligent in the observance of order, a companion of females, a lover of horses, soon angry, eager at detracting, incorrigible in all things.' What is more, he was just out of imprisonment for mis-behaviour at a Canterbury monastery – but he stayed as Abbot of Evesham for twenty-two years until deposed by the Papal Legate.

John's successor, his eldest son Henry, who ruled for fifty-six years as Henry III, was the basic cause for Evesham's next great trouble, the famous battle seven years before his death. He and the great lords fell out about the interpretation of Magna Carta and how the land should be governed, and in the Barons' War that followed he was taken into what we could call 'protective custody' at the Battle of Lewes in 1264. Simon de Montfort, who has been described as 'the father of

69

English liberty' because he called the first Parliament at which merchants and traders were present as well as barons and bishops, was entrusted with his care.

The King's son and heir (who later became Edward I, 'Hammer of the Scots' and the Welsh, too), had also been taken prisoner and was confined at de Montfort's stronghold of Kenilworth Castle. But not all the barons were against the royal family, and Roger de Mortimer, sixth of the line which reached such heights in the Welsh Marches, planned the prince's escape – and provided the horse on which he made it. Edward raised an army and by the summer of 1265 had de Montfort (who had the King with him) pinned down on the Severn at Kempsey, just south of Worcester.

Then a spy reported that the garrison at Kenilworth had grown slack. Edward, at 26 a fighting man in his prime, drove his army on a fantastic march. He raced to Kenilworth from Worcester (which he left on the morning of Sunday, August 2), captured Kenilworth, and was back again nearing Evesham by the morning of Tuesday, August 4 – sixty miles in forty-eight hours!

He had caught the Earl in the equivalent of a fisherman's net. When he learnt Edward had gone, de Montfort had crossed the Severn and headed for Kenilworth, hoping to catch his foe between his own army and the Kenilworth garrison, commanded by his own son, the younger Simon. But through Henry III insisting on hearing mass at Kempsey and Evesham Abbey (and perhaps some complacency), he was still at Evesham on that fateful Tuesday morning when an army was reported approaching from the north. At first he thought the troops were his men from Kenilworth, particularly since they were carrying his banners. Then he saw it was Edward's army, carrying captured colours as a subterfuge. He is supposed to have turned to his other son, Henry, and said: 'Commend our souls to God, for our bodies are theirs.'

It was a general's stoic acceptance of the situation. The de Montfort army was inside the loop of the Avon where Evesham stands. Edward had troops on the other side of the river – and he was attacking downhill, with far more men.

The fighting began where the road from Alcester enters Evesham, on the slopes of Green Hill. It raged for three hours in a thunderstorm. Then de Montfort was killed by men commanded by Roger de Mortimer. Vengeance was wreaked on his corpse. The arms and legs were cut off, to be sent to various parts of the country to show that the Earl was dead; the severed head was sent by Mortimer as a trophy to his wife at the family stronghold, then at Wigmore in Herefordshire; there was more mutilation, and at last the monks gathered up what little remained and buried them in front of the abbey's high altar.

The cause seemed lost. De Montfort's son Henry had also been killed, with 18 barons, 160 knights and some

4,000 soldiers. But Earl Simon became a folk hero, and more people flocked to his tomb than even St Egwin had drawn. And that went on, with Evesham assured of a ready trade in pilgrims, until the Dissolution, when the abbey became, in effect, a ready-made stone quarry for those wanting to build. There was no hope of reprieve, as at Tewkesbury, because the town had other churches to serve the religious needs of the people.

But the site of Earl Simon's tomb was not forgotten, and in 1965, to mark the seven hundredth anniversary of his death, a suitably inscribed stone dedicated by the Archbishop of Canterbury was erected in the correct place and unveiled by the Speaker of the House of Commons.

There is another de Montfort memorial in Evesham, although not generally available for the public to see. It is an obelisk in the grounds of Abbey Manor, near where the battle began. It shows the incident in which Henry III, on the ground with a man with an upraised sword over him, cried 'Do not kill me, I am your King.'

This approach down Green Hill seems to make the most of Evesham. It broadens into the well-treed High Street which sets the scene for the riverside parks stretching along the Avon's banks and providing an enormous amount of space for families, particularly those with boating interests. And it has a wealth of attractive houses and shops which give an air of easy opulence – with one in particular that is outstanding.

This is No. 51, Dresden House, which dates from 1692 if an elaborate lead rainwater head can be trusted. It is a house to grace any town, five bays of mellowed brick, with what Pevsner describes as 'glorious big iron brackets' at the front door. If you wonder at such a name deep in the heart of Worcestershire, it formerly belonged to a doctor whose financial straits forced him to live in Dresden, where he became physician to Frederick the Great, King of Prussia.

Another name with a history crops up where High Street narrows to Tudor and medieval buildings. The eye-catcher is a great black-and-white house isolated among busy streets, with heavy vertical timbering and now occupied by a bank. It is the Booth House or the Round House – which seems strange for a four-sided building until you find out that the second name goes back to at least 1582 and denotes 'the old inn sign of premises around which one can walk'.

Many of Evesham's best buildings are those of old inns, such as the Crown, in Bridge Street, the narrow street of shops that goes down to Evesham's older bridge. The most dramatic way to approach Evesham Abbey and its associated buildings is through Abbot Reginald's Gateway, along an obscure-looking alley to the left of the Booth House as approached from High Street.

There are *two* parish churches only a few yards from each other – a constant headache for maintenance. All

71

Evesham Round House – although it is in fact four-sided. It is now used as a bank

Saints is Norman and the older, and was the one used by Evesham parishioners; St Lawrence's, built nearly three hundred years later, was supposedly intended for pilgrims, in case they brought in plague. Each contains a memorial to Evesham's last true abbot, Clement Lichfield. He is buried in the former, in the Lichfield Chapel, and the latter has the chantry chapel of St Clement. Each

has a beautiful vaulted stone roof. But the gem of the area stands between them and a little nearer the river. It is the bell-tower that Abbot Clement had built to stand free of the abbey buildings and which had only just been completed when the dissolution of the monastery was announced. It is one of the most lavish Perpendicular buildings that exists, 110 feet high, pierced by a gateway. Near it is the de Montfort statue already mentioned and then the parkland sweeps down to the Avon with little more than one crumbling arch to show that the famous abbey stood there.

Back in Vine Street, along another tree-lined walk, is the almonry, used in abbey times to distribute alms to the needy. Now the half-timbered building houses the local museum, imaginatively laid out in the range of differently shaped rooms and in the courtyard at the back. One of the most impressive items is the huge carved chair which was used by the abbots of Evesham and dates back to about 1335. On the lawns outside the almonry are the town's old stocks, given a roof of Cotswold stone slabs when re-erected after many years as the town hall jail house, and on the other side of the road is what used to be the old grammar school (converted to a working men's club). Carved on its stonework is still another reminder of the famous abbot – an inscription just possible to read on the stone porch 'Orate pro anima Clementis Abbatis' ('Pray for the soul of Abbot Clement').

The two parish churches at Evesham, dominated by the Abbot's Bell-tower

The stocks and almonry – which is now the town museum, Evesham

The Abbot's Gateway at Evesham

There was another Battle of Evesham, although there is no public trace. It took place during the Civil War when Evesham was a vital link in the King's communications between his headquarters at Oxford and his sources of supply in Wales and the Welsh border. Colonel Edward Massey, Governor of Parliamentary-held Gloucester, attacked the town on May 26, 1645, with about two thousand men against a garrison of seven hundred, who were not enough to man earthworks across the loop of the Avon, again at Green Hill. Massey attacked the earthworks at five separate places, broke in only to be twice repulsed, and was about to be driven out for the third time in fierce fighting when, in the same tactical way that Cromwell used later at Worcester, a sixth detachment forced the river bridge, stormed up Bridge Street, and the Royalist garrison, caught between two fires, surrendered.

Now Evesham's battles are commercial ones – the prices of the vegetables and fruit from the market gardens that fill the landscape for miles around. Perhaps the best time of all is the spring, especially in those years when the fruit blossom breaks before the leaf and the plum orchards seem like a massive Milky Way brought down to earth. The pick-it-yourself boom has brought fresh impetus to growing, too. There seems to be a competition to find ever more crops that city people can come out to pick. One firm alone advertises more than twenty, including such exotics as green peppers. This means cultivation under cover and everywhere can be seen what seem to be small aircraft hangars of polythene. But even this cannot detract from the rich beauty of this fertile landscape.

The National Trust has been taking a great interest in this area. At Middle Littleton, three miles north-east of Evesham, it spent £60,000 over six years in the 1970s in restoring a thirteenth-century tithe barn with a roof of Cotswold-stone tiles and 136 feet long. And at Bretforton, the same distance due east, the Fleece was the third public house the Trust took over, after the death in 1977 of the licensee, 83-year-old Miss Lola Taplow, licensee and owner since her mother died thirty years before. The half-timbered building was a farmhouse before it was licensed in the middle of the nineteenth century, and was in the same family for more than five hundred years. And a little further round this eastern circle of Evesham is Wickhamford, with a brook dancing through orchards and meadows past a church where, within the altar rails, is a stone to a relative of George Washington, bearing the Washington arms of stars and stripes which became the basis for the American flag (although with nothing like so many of either).

Southwards the Avon flows past Cropthorne, a pretty black-and-white village across the river from Fladbury – in its church is a cross-head which is the finest piece of Anglo-Saxon art in Worcestershire – to the urbane township of Pershore. There red-brick Georgian houses stretch down to the river in the same pleasantly condescending way that a ruddy-faced gentleman farmer would survey his land.

The buildings have a mellowed confidence with hardly anything more recent than Georgian in the main street (which is first Bridge Street and then High Street). Those on the east side back on to the Avon. Perrott House, built for a Baron of the Exchequer in 1760, is generally regarded as the best, although the Three Tuns Inn in Broad Street is notable. This is more of a market square than a street. Perhaps something happened with the dissolution of the abbey, which is the real reason for Pershore's existence. The abbey was one of the cluster established in the fertile Severn-Avon valleys area in Saxon times – the others were Worcester and Gloucester (now cathedrals) and Tewkesbury and Evesham.

Pershore escaped more lightly at the hands of Henry VIII's men than Evesham, but only because the townspeople paid £400 to save the choir (above which rises the stately tower) and the transepts. For this reason, compared with the towering height of the stone fan-vaulting, which is better than that of many a cathedral, Pershore's parish church, once part of the abbey, seems small in ground area. Two large fires in the thirteenth century meant major rebuilding in the Decorated style, but there is an elaborately carved Norman font which was turned out when a new font was presented in 1840 and spent the next eighty years as a garden ornament!

The Royal Three Tuns at Pershore, with its famous wrought-iron balcony

The part of Pershore Abbey that was bought at the Reformation to serve as the parish church

Pershore is nationally known for something more material than its abbey, though. One of the great names in plums is the Pershore Egg Plum, which comes in both yellow and purple varieties. It is more of a cooker than an eater, and a lot of the orchards have been grubbed up for dessert varieties – but the plum is still popular enough for a public house on a new housing estate to be named after it.

Just west of Pershore, the Avon swings southwards to run at a gradually narrowing angle with the Severn. The corridor between the rivers is not seven miles at its widest, yet into it have been squeezed the A38, the old trunk road from Derby to Bristol, the Birmingham to Bristol railway and the M5 motorway, plus the M50 junction. Again a large-scale map is necessary to go exploring, but it is well worth it.

Three miles west of Pershore, for instance, is the tiny picturesque church of Besford, the only surviving half-timbered church in the county. The oak dates back to the fourteenth century having escaped not only the weather but the attentions of restorers and reformers. In 1880 it was treated with sympathy by a Victorian restorer, and in the times of the Reformation the complete rood loft parapet survived too.

Pirton church, on the other side of the railway line, retains its timber-framed tower, too. At Kempsey, being overrun by houses for Worcester commuters, the church has a photograph of a chestnut tree that grew *inside* it for ninety years. Three miles south along the A38, at Severn Stoke, the stair-turret of the 700-year-old tower is higher than the tower-top itself. Earl's Croome, where the present Earl of Coventry lives at the timber-framed court, also has a Norman church. And Ripple, Worcestershire's southernmost village on Severnside, pinned in between the river, the M50 and the A38, has in its large church a set of misericords depicting one of the few complete sets in England of The Twelve Labours of the Months – a favourite medieval subject, recalling the curse laid on Adam: 'In the sweat of thy face shalt thou eat bread'. The labours include sowing in March, scything in June and feeding acorns to pigs in October.

Hemmed in between the M5 and the railway is Croome d'Abitot, the name of which perpetuates that of Urse d'Abitot, on whom William the Conqueror bestowed Worcester (there is also a Redmarley d'Abitot, in Gloucestershire just south of the M50). The estate was bought in 1592 by Thomas Coventry, a rich Elizabethan merchant, and the earldom was created just over a century later. The sixth earl called in Lancelot ('Capability') Brown to produce a house and parkland appropriate to the family. The result was a stately home ranking with anything on the Welsh Marches – but family deaths and estate duties, plus a Second World War RAF station, have taken their toll. The court passed into use as a school, and is not open to the ordinary visitor, and Capability's grounds and their 'park furnishings' – such as temple, grotto, tower, summer house, rotunda and even sham Norman castle ruin – are in a bad way. As for perhaps the most splendid 'eye-catcher' of all, St Mary Magdalene's, on a brow to the north, that is in the care of the Redundant Churches Fund.

The Croome Estates office is helpful with information where to find the key – but the way to the church provides a shock. It lies through the bedraggled remnants of RAF huts, and is a thorough disgrace, leading as it does to a most unusual church, excellently maintained although no longer in use. Inside is delicate Georgian building work at its best in the body of the church, but into the chancel is crowded a most overpowering collection of massive marble monuments. The sixth earl certainly assembled the family there, including himself.

That leaves just one part of this lower Avon area to explore – Bredon Hill, which broods over the Vale of Evesham like a friendly old bear, with its head hunched down between heavy shoulders. Surrounding the hill is a chaplet of villages, seeming to have been placed artistically on their sites, but really there for a thoroughly practical reason.

Bredon, although not all that high – just under one thousand feet – dominates the countryside for miles around. Experts on place-names say that its impression on men down the ages has been so great that it is one of the few places that carry the same name in two different languages: the 'bre' is from the Celtic 'brigs' and the 'don' from the Old English 'tun' (each meaning 'hill'). It is the largest Cotswold outlier, about 3½ miles long and 1½ wide, and it is basically a big bed of limestone dipping down from a steep escarpment at the north. Underlying this is a bed of clay, and that gives the mundane reason for the siting of the villages: they are where springs burst out.

The hill remains unspoilt largely because its gradient has discouraged road-builders, so to reach the top, by any number of footpaths from all sides, calls for a longish uphill walk. But the view is outstanding, across Housman's 'coloured counties' to the Malverns and Wales in the west, the Cotswolds to the south and along the whole fertile Avon valley. There are as well the remains of an Iron Age camp, where, for the macabre-minded, fifty-five skeletons were found hacked to pieces when it was excavated; the stone tower known as Parsons' Folly, which has nothing to do with clergymen but a local worthy, Mr Parsons, who had it built towards the end of the eighteenth century; and the strange rocks called the Banbury Stone and the King and Queen stones, that protrude through the surface. These are really great blocks of natural concrete, made down the ages by fragments of limestone falling into clefts and then being cemented together by petrifying water, forming material more resistant to erosion than the natural stone.

The picture-postcard village of Elmley Castle, at the north-east of the hill is a favourite one, as much for the approach as for how enjoyable it is to walk around. The eleventh-century castle from which the village takes its name ceased to exist nearly five hundred years ago, and now Elmley is the epitome of peace. A tree-lined main street with a clear stream bubbling at the side straggles between half-timbered thatched cottages and old brick houses and past the Queen Elizabeth Inn (she visited Elmley on August 20, 1575) to the medieval church which has two widely famous memorials to 'big' families – and a homelier one to a vicar's wife who died in childbirth in 1609. The excellent guide to the church comments: 'This must be one of the earliest memorials to a vicar's wife, as pre-Reformation clergy were not permitted to marry.' It also points out that the massive porch door, when made in 1636, cost eighteen shillings, plus ten pence to fit!

Three miles south along the minor road beside the church is Ashton-under-Hill, a long straggling village with a Norman nave in its church, an almost complete fifteenth-century cross and imposing farmhouses, but since 1977 most notable as being appointed 'Ambridge' by the BBC for the world's longest-running radio serial, *The Archers*. Ashton's pub, The Star, becomes The Bull for Ambridge purposes.

At Beckford, where excavations have proved human habitation for more than two thousand years, the church's tympanum represents an apocryphal fifth-century legend about Christ 'harrowing Hell' by going there and rescuing Adam. The primitive Norman carving shows Jesus opening the mouth of Hell (represented by a leviathan) with his cross so that Adam can follow him.

Up a lane leading north, through Conderton, is Bredon's other Iron Age earthworks, known as Danes Camp. This is limestone country, with iron impurities making the soil a russet colour, excellent for barley growing, and the fields are getting bigger and bigger, extending to as much as eighty acres at Overbury, delightful even among Bredon villages. Stuart, Georgian and Victorian houses merge together in a richness of stone and half-timbered houses and buildings. And then, through pretty but featureless Kemerton, is Bredon village itself.

The other way to Bredon, anti-clockwise round the hill, takes in more villages, following the snaking course of the Avon. Bricklehampton, rich with orcharding, leads to the Combertons – Great Comberton full of thatch and old-world gardens, with a vast dovecote with 1,425 nest-holes; Little Comberton (which is in fact the larger of the villages nowadays) with two dovecotes, although they are smaller ones, and a church with a tympanum that Pevsner describes as 'very strange', with a 'cross of bulgy whorls, four left and four right'.

Birlingham is hardly a Bredon village, because it is cut off in a great loop on the other bank of the Avon, but it is well worth visiting, particularly in spring, because the snowdrops and crocuses in its churchyard are noted locally. Then the narrow fifteenth-century Eckington bridge, preceded by notices warning of flooding, with cutwaters giving vantage points to see the pleasure boats thronging the river, through Eckington village to Bredon's Norton, up a by-lane off the main road, but worth searching for at the foot of the hill's western slopes, with an old tithe barn converted into the village hall. Two impressive houses stand at the outskirts, and although neither is open to the public, the one called Norton Park is worth recalling as the home, until her death in the 1920s, of a remarkable American woman named Victoria, who came to England when nearly 40, married a banker and settled down, after a stormy life in the States which ranged from advocating Women's Lib and 'free love' in the 1860s to founding a newspaper, becoming New York's first female stockbroker and being the first woman candidate for the US Presidency with a policy that included equal rights for women. To think that she settled down in a place so far away from it all as Bredon's Norton!

Road, railway and river all isolate Strensham from the Bredon villages. Indeed, now it is known to most only as a place where there is a service station on the M5, close to the M50 junction. Yet it is a charming village where there is the base of a medieval cross, a moated castle-site, and mellowed seventeenth-century almshouses. The church, standing alone in fields overlooking the Avon, is not much to look at but has a wealth of interesting furnishings, including some 500-year-old folk-paintings of twenty-three saints which probably formed part of the former rood screen. There is also a memorial to the poet Samuel Butler, who was born at Strensham Court and whose 'Hudibras', satirizing the Puritans and written while he was a tutor at Ludlow Castle, was favourite reading of Charles II after the Restoration. The King gave away many copies, although it makes singularly dull reading nowadays. I ploughed through it once and remember a brace of couplets as standing out from the rest. The Puritans: 'Thought fire, sword and conflagration a thorough Godly reformation' and 'prove their doctrine orthodox by apostolic blows and knocks'.

This leaves Bredon village itself of the communities nestling in the shadow of the great hill that is still used by the vale farmers to forecast weather. When the top is shrouded in cloud, rain is coming – 'when Bredon Hill puts on his hat, ye men of the Vale beware of that'. Some two thousand people live in Bredon, making it almost a township, although modern housing has not been allowed to affect the impression created by the street of old houses and more ambitious buildings leading to and around the high-spired church. Not many churches in this area have a spire, let alone such a splendid one as this, which dominates the countryside around with its 160-foot peak. Memorials inside a rich interior include a brass to Bishop Prideaux, who came to live in Bredon with his son-in-law, then the rector, after being dispossessed as Bishop of Worcester during the Civil War. For a saintly man, he had expensive tastes, and although he sold what personal possessions remained to him, including his books, he died worth only a few shillings.

He lived at the Rectory, which looks more like a bishop's palace than some I have seen, an Elizabethan building so large that it is on record that one incumbent had fifteen servants and fires in eighteen rooms. On the roof two figures seem to be firing at each other with cannons. They represent Charles I and Cromwell, and local legend says that if they ever meet, the rectory will collapse; little wonder, because the roof's main supporting beam would go.

Other buildings around the church include the brick-built Old Mansion and, west of St Giles's the five-bayed stone manor house. Down a path through the churchyard is Bredon's second most famous building, its tithe barn. This has been owned by the National Trust since 1951, and is only four feet shorter than the more recently acquired one at Middle Littleton, mentioned earlier. Regrettably, it was badly damaged by fire in 1980.

Back in the main street, the single-storeyed Reed Almshouses built in 1696 have to be admired (there is a Reed family memorial in the church) and nearby is the half-timbered Fox and Hounds. The talk there is mainly about boats, because the moorings on the Avon's banks are now a major feature of Bredon. This is the pub that was especially favoured by author John Moore, whose books about 'Brensham' (a fictitious village with a name of easily deduced origin) were turned into a television series by the BBC in the late 1970s.

John came from Tewkesbury, which is Gloucestershire – Bredon is Worcestershire. But the two counties join so imperceptibly here that official boundaries do not seem to matter. For instance, two miles west of Bredon is Twyning, Gloucestershire's most northerly village, isolated in a kind of oasis by the Avon and the Severn, both the motorways and the A38. Only a minor road leads to its timber-framed cottages and its Norman church. North-west in a wood only a few yards south of the M50, just before the bridge over the Severn, is an Iron Age hill-fort which covered twenty acres before quarrying partially destroyed it. And less than two miles south lies the third battlefield, Tewkesbury.

CHAPTER SIX

From Abbey to Priory

Tewkesbury is a classic example of getting a quart of town into a pint pot of land, with a site limited by a combination of natural and man-made obstacles.

Eastward expansion was limited because the land belonged to the great feudal owner of the Honour of Tewkesbury (an 'honour' being a holding so large that it took in several manors) or to the abbey that is the reason for the town's being.

Elsewhere water makes the boundary – and provides the setting for the third of the battlefields. The Avon joins the Severn just south of the town, on land so low-lying and liable to flooding that it was not until early last century that the Severn was bridged here. And other small rivers and streams ooze through lush water-meadows so fertile that the Benedictines established a monastery here some 1,200 years ago, during their great settlement of the lower Severn and Avon valleys.

William the Conqueror seized it immediately after the Conquest as a personal possession for his Queen Matilda, who wanted it to spite its Saxon owner who had refused her when he was an envoy from Edward the Confessor to her father's court. William retained it after her death, and it passed on in royal possession.

Later, great lords became its owners, and did not encourage efforts to build on their land, so by the late Middle Ages pressure on the site had become so intense that alleyways were being driven through the fronts of buildings facing the three main streets, using their gardens and backlands for more houses.

It is only in this century that there has been any notable increase in the site's size, with the result that the old part of Tewkesbury can be covered on foot in an astonishingly short time, with continual glimpses of medieval alleys and courts. In some of them the overhanging buildings almost touch.

The best place to get an overall idea of this is from the top of the tower of the famous abbey, classed by Alec Clifton-Taylor in a BBC television series in 1978 called *Six English Towns* as the 'third finest English church not a cathedral' (the top rankings, Westminster Abbey and

Beverley Minster, Yorkshire). There are 205 steps to the battlements, which provide a view worth every bit of the exertion. Tewkesbury is laid out like a map 130 feet below, with the unusual Y-shaped street pattern easy to follow. The road from Gloucester splits at the High Cross into a left arm for Evesham and the Midlands and a right one for the Cotswolds and London.

The Avon runs a couple of hundred yards to the west with the Severn just beyond, divided from it by the great water-meadow of Severn Ham. Southwards, almost in the shadow of the abbey, runs the little strangely named River Swilgate. Beyond it, swampy-looking land rises to gentle well-treed heights, now Tewkesbury Park, with a modern housing estate creeping across from the east.

It was here and over that hill that the Battle of Tewkesbury, one of the bloodiest of even the Wars of the Roses, was fought on May 4, 1471, when Edward IV snuffed out the red rose of Lancaster.

In much the same manoeuvre as that used at Evesham, he caught his enemies with their backs to the Severn and the little Swilgate, and when they broke, as many drowned as were slain by sword, lance and arrow. Some sought refuge in Tewkesbury town, some in the abbey – but they were hunted down. Prominent prisoners were court martialled the next day with Edward's 21-year-old brother, Richard of Gloucester (later Richard III), presiding as Constable of England; many were beheaded immediately at the High Cross.

Tewkesbury Abbey is full of memorials to notable Lancastrians who were killed in the battle or executed after it (at least their bodies were more humanely treated than that of Simon de Montfort at Evesham). Perhaps the most poignant is a brass in the floor of the choir, immediately under the massive tower, to Henry VI's only son, Edward. It says: 'Here lies Edward Prince of Wales, cruelly slain whilst but a youth, on May 4, 1471. Alas, the savagery of men! Thou art the sole light of thy mother and the last hope of thy race'. There is another side to the coin – a contemporary diplomatic report to the Duke of Milan: 'This boy, although only 13 years of age, already talks of nothing but of cutting off heads or making war, as if he had everything in his hands or was the god of battle . . .'. They bred savage boys as well as savage youths in those times!

Nor did they forget enmities easily. The vaulted roof above the memorial brass is decorated with gilded suns – the Yorkist badge of the sun in splendour looking down on the last Lancastrian heir as long as the abbey abides.

The abbey itself is often called 'The Westminster Abbey of feudal baronage', because of the magnificence of its memorials to medieval nobles. The first impression, after entering through massively crude doors that are believed to be the original ones of 1123, is somewhat claustrophobic because a fourteenth-century benefactor decided that the timber-roof crowning the mighty round piers of the nave should be replaced by stone fan-vaulting. This gives a squashed-down effect, but it is a different story east of the nave where the medieval masons used Cotswold stone in making one of the most glorious roofs in the country.

The only way to appreciate Tewkesbury Abbey is at leisure, with guidebook in hand. It ranges from the magnificent to the macabre. Outside, not far from the awesome west front, at sixty-five feet the tallest Norman arch in England, is stonework still faintly red because of a great fire in 1178. Inside, the seven windows that give light to Prince Edward's monument are among the finest fourteenth-century glass in the country, and a few yards away, the inner side of the sacristy door is strengthened by pieces of armour, hammered flat, taken from those killed in the battle. The exquisite carving of the Despenser Chapel has near it the gruesome Wakeman Cenotaph, which contains a stone statue of a corpse with the vermin of the grave crawling over it. Beneath an iron grating is the entrance to the tomb of George, Duke of Clarence, who fought at the side of his brothers, Edward IV and Richard III (as he later became), but whose conduct became such that he was personally denounced by the king for treason, committed to the Tower of London and never seen alive again; Shakespeare has it that 'false, fleeting, perjured Clarence' was drowned in a butt of Malmsey wine.

All this only scratches the surface of the quirks of humanity to be seen in the abbey, which exists now only because Tewkesbury's citizens bought the building when Henry VIII dissolved the monasteries in 1539. The price was fixed at the value of the lead on the roof and the metal in the bells (£311 for the lead and £142 for the bell metal) and the total of £453 was paid to Henry VIII in person in three instalments.

Tewkesbury saw more military action during the Civil War, when between them the Royalists and the Parliamentarians occupied and reoccupied it eight times, but it escaped any great damage. It remained a quiet market town, relying mainly on its river traffic, until 1823, when the great architect Thomas Telford bridged the Severn near the town's only previous bridge, the one that King John had had built across the Avon. There had been no Severn bridge before because the river bed was too soft for piers, but Telford used the techniques that had been pioneered at Ironbridge and crossed the river with a single span of cast iron 170-foot long, floated downstream from Shropshire.

The new bridge meant that Tewkesbury had a main road running east and west as well as north and south, and before long it was a major coaching centre. As many as thirty coaches a day were using it, bringing great prosperity through travellers needing overnight accommodation. The town even got a free 'plug' through Dickens, who had Mr Pickwick stop at the Hop Pole in *Pickwick Papers* while on his way from Bristol to Birmingham to break the news to Mr Winkle's father of

Tewkesbury Abbey, encrusted with chantry chapels

his son's marriage. The hotel, which has added a 'Royal' to its name, is just up Church Street from the abbey, with a round plaque at the right-hand side of the main entrance giving the relevant extract: 'At the Hop Pole at Tewkesbury they stopped to dine; upon which occasion there was more bottled ale, with some more Madeira, and some Port besides; and here the case bottle was replenished for the fourth time. Under the influence of these combined stimulants, Mr Pickwick and Mr Ben Allen fell asleep for 30 miles . . .'

Church Street, which is the main road from Gloucester, has some outstanding buildings in it, notably the half-timbered Bell Inn, which is much older than the 1696 carved on its front. At its side is a narrow road leading to the old Abbey Mill (now a restaurant), other half-timbered buildings, and the moorings and boatyards clustered along Avon banks. The next narrow street has one of the oldest Baptist chapels and burial grounds with a deed dated 1623. Back in Church Street are other good houses, among them Craik House, formerly the home of Mrs Dinah Maria Craik, a Victorian novelist who wrote *John Halifax, Gentleman*, the story of an orphan who achieved success after overcoming many adversities. It is set in Tewkesbury, and was a 'vogue' book for so many years that Mrs Craik's name occurs time and time again in Tewkesbury guides.

Left at the High Cross – now occupied by a World Wars memorial – is Tewkesbury's main shopping street, and

Tewkesbury's Bell Hotel, one of the town's most noted half-timbered buildings

also a less obvious memorial to the town's more recent famous writer. John Moore, mentioned in the last chapter, was born in Tewkesbury, a member of a well-known family firm – referred to in an inscription on the window of No. 46 as: 'Moore & Sons, Established 1751, Auction and Estate Offices'.

Locally made Georgian brick, dating back to the prosperous coaching times, is a feature of many of the large hotels and houses in the street, but there is spectacular

88

half-timbering, too, notably the Tudor House Hotel, with its Queen Anne staircase, and the House of the Nodding Gables, four storeys of overhanging old oak and plaster. Topping the building are twin gables that seem in peril of lurching down at any time, but they are safe and sound; what happened was that the ridge-pieces broke many years ago, and extra securing had to be fitted.

The town map shows a maze of narrow medieval streets backing on High Street's east side, but a new shopping precinct with the necessary car parks has broken the spell. To savour the old atmosphere, it is best to push on to the other main road forking off at the High Cross. This is Barton Street, so called because it led to the barton (a word derived from 'barley' and meaning granary) of the feudal lord. Main features include the town's museum, housed in a carefully restored seventeenth-century building with a continuous stretch of leaded-light casement windows at first floor level, and the less striking-looking No. 13, a reminder of one of Tewkesbury's old industries. It is called the Mustard House and it is believed that mustard seed was dried on its smooth upper-storey floor before being ground and prepared into balls which were sent to all parts of the country. Tewkesbury mustard was supposed to be extra hot and biting. Men looking very strong were often described as looking as if they lived on it, and Shakespeare, in a scene from *Henry IV Part II*, has Falstaff

The House of the Nodding Gables, Tewkesbury

say of Poins: 'His wit is as thick as Tewkesbury mustard'.

South of Tewkesbury is the Saxon priory church of Deerhurst. This survived a Danish sacking from which only one monk survived, and he fled to Malvern, that great dinosaur of a range of hills beckoning from the north-west. The road to Malvern leads past the Black Bear, founded in 1308 and the oldest inn in Gloucestershire, and over King John's Bridge, which is really two bridges, rebuilt and widened in 1962 but still retaining some of the original stonework. It then runs across Telford's Mythe Bridge and back into an area of Worcestershire which resembles no other part of that county.

The Ice Age brought down vast quantities of fragmented stone to form gravel beds – claimed to be the best gravel in Europe because it is extremely hard and carries practically no dust. It consists of stones polished by rubbing against each other all the way from the Scottish Highlands to the Worcestershire part of the Severn Valley. This glaciation has resulted in a hummocky countryside interspersed with flat stretches of poor-quality soil that have become commons and provide poor grazing. The largest is Castlemorton, covering something like six hundred acres. Because the living is sparse, so are houses and villages. But this helps in providing spectacular views of the Malvern Hills, particularly when the sun is setting behind them.

East of the hills, as they tail off southwards into Chase End and Midsummer Hill is Birtsmorton, with its historic court where the young Wolsey started the career that led to his high office with Henry VIII; Castlemorton, with remains of its castle visible south of the church; and Longdon, with an eye-catching half-timbered house. Welland has, of all things, a font in a glass case; it is a seventeenth-century one, retained when the church was rebuilt in 1875, and is only ten inches high – unusually small for the period.

Upton-on-Severn, once the key centre for all this area, is regaining through pleasure-boating the importance it had before the railways changed the nation's transport system. Until Telford's bridge at Tewkesbury, it had the only bridge across the Severn between Gloucester and Worcester, and was such a meeting-place for trading craft plying the river that what was known as the Bridge Parliament was held there. But by the middle of the nineteenth century, its trade faded out and, as at Tewkesbury, little has been built in the old streets since Georgian times.

An indirect result of this is that Upton has more old inns per head of resident population than most places – although this comes in handy for the pleasure trade. There is the White Lion, for instance, where novelist Henry Fielding set several scenes in *Tom Jones*. The Anchor is half-timbered, the Bell has its sign in copper, there are also the Talbot, the Swan and the Star. Not a

The Anchor, one of Upton-on-Severn's picturesque inns

bad basis for a resident population of not more than two thousand.

The present bridge is a handsome single-span, completed just before the Second World War. It had at least three predecessors, about one of which a story of great bravery has come down from the Civil War.

When Charles II made Worcester his headquarters in 1651, the Royalists blew out sections of various bridges to prevent being outflanked. Among them was Upton, with two of its four spans blown. But a negligent guard went off drinking in the Anchor instead of doing their duty, and what is more left a plank bridging the gap, although their orders had been to remove it. In a seventeenth-century commando-style raid, something like a dozen Roundheads crawled across the plank and barricaded themselves in the church. By the time the Royalists were attacking them there, Parliamentary horse were pouring across a ford left undefended, and there was hand-to-hand fighting, in which the Royalists got the worst of it and had to abandon Upton.

The damaged church was rebuilt in the mid eighteenth-century, and this in its turn was replaced by a Victorian one in 1875. The remains of the old church were demolished in 1937 – all except the tower, which stands alone close to the Severn. It dates back some seven hundred years, but is surmounted by a copper-covered cupola on an eight-sided mounting. It is about two hundred years old and looks so un-English that it has many nicknames, of which The Pepperpot is perhaps the most flattering.

Nearby, at the corner of New Street, is a stone pillar marking the site of the town's ducking stool, used for four centuries for ducking 'slanderous women' in a nearby 'dirty pool'.

A mile north-west of Upton are the traces of what used to be the most important place in the area – Hanley Castle. A few hummocks and depressions just south of the church in the picture-book village represent all that remains of the castle from which the great

91

hunting area between the Severn and the Malverns was administered.

Malvern Forest was a royal possession for many years. King John loved to hunt in it and had the castle built as a very superior hunting lodge. Then the territory passed to the de Clares with the Honour of Tewkesbury (where several of them are buried in the abbey). One of them, the Gilbert known as the Red Earl, was a specially fiery example. Hunted deer do not worry about boundaries and Gilbert became increasingly angry when animals he

The village green at Hanley Castle – where no trace remains of the castle that was a royal hunting lodge

was after crossed over to the western side of the Malverns, where the Bishop of Hereford held the hunting rights. His patience became so exhausted that, around 1287, he had a ditch dug along the spine of the Malverns, probably following a much older track, and also installed a palisade to prevent the deer leaping out of his territory. It survives as the Red Earl's Dyke, and until the two counties were joined by local government re-organization in 1974, still formed part of the boundary between Herefordshire and Worcestershire.

Hanley Castle remained a place of great importance as the official residence of the Keeper of Malvern Forest (with the power of life and death) until Tudor times, when it was pulled down as part of Henry VII's policy of reducing the power of the barons. Stone from it was used for rebuilding in the area around. Now it seems ironic that buildings meant to serve it, such as the half-timbered almshouses and grammar school, remain clustered around the village green and its huge cedar tree.

Neighbouring Hanley Swan has two churches, an Anglican one by Sir George Gilbert Scott and a Roman Catholic one built thirty years earlier in 1846, of which Pevsner comments: '. . . remarkably stately. One feels nowhere the pinch of poverty which mars so much of Catholic architecture in England before 1850.' Newland, on the road from Malvern to Worcester, has St Leonard's, completed in 1864, where the walls, the roof and even the organ, are painted with subjects including miracles, parables and the Beatitudes.

High Victorian, all of it – and that sets the theme for Malvern itself, a collection of townships sited where springs gush out of the mountainside, much as at Bredon. They were little more than villages until the quality of the Malvern water and the coming of the railway made them popular. Then they grew fast – as they are still growing with the influx of commuters to Worcester and people finding a pleasant spot for retirement.

The story of the Malvern water cure is so remarkable that books and countless articles have been written about it. It is astounding the lengths to which people will go in pursuit of health and fashion. Briefly, it began when the Dr John Wall who founded the Royal Worcester Porcelain Works decided there was business, too, in Malvern water. The problem was, though, that spas such as Bath, Cheltenham, Harrogate and so on were renowned for the very unpleasantness of the taste of their waters, in which the curative properties were supposed to lie, whereas Malvern water was sparklingly pure and pleasant to drink. Undeterred, he pressed on with a campaign that sounds strange nowadays – that because the water was so pure, it could pass through 'the vessels of the body' better than other waters and so effect cures.

When he retired – to Bath, of all places! – Malvern was growing as a spa, and by the turn of the eighteenth century such still-flourishing hotels as the Foley Arms were replacing places such as 'John Dugard's Lodging House'. Malvern was flourishing, and the stay of the future Queen Victoria with her mother, the Duchess of Kent, in 1830, did nothing but help. Ten-year-old Victoria often rode up the hills on a donkey soon widely known as 'Royal Moses'.

Great Malvern was the hub of it all, then as now, with activity centred on the Bellevue Terrace, overlooking the ancient priory. Samuel and John Deykes, father and son, provided such spa essentials as the Coburg Baths (with pump room) and the Royal Library. Although neither is now used for its original purpose, they still stand to give Georgian grace, style and light. Then the Deykeses went on with hotels, spacious villas and footpaths, and drives along the slopes of the hills giving unparalleled views.

The next leap forward began in 1842, with the arrival of Dr James Wilson and Dr J. M. Gully who had both been greatly impressed by a drastic water cure practised at a Czechoslovakian spa by a Dr Preissnitz. They had decided that Malvern, with its pure and exceptionally cold water, was just the place for a similar establishment.

By any standards the treatment was terrifying. It consisted of cold baths, spending hours motionless bandaged in wringing wet sheets, even enduring douches which included cascading fifty gallons of icy water from a height on to an unsuspecting naked human being, male or female, clutching a rail below. Add to that a rigid diet, no relaxations of any kind (including reading), and a daily climb up the Malverns, going from well to well and drinking as much as possible. The wonder is that any patients survived. Yet it was the thing to do, so many people wanted to take the treatment at the Hydropathic Establishment the two doctors had set up. This was first at the Crown Hotel (near the side of which a footpath starts to the most famous of all Malvern's wells, St Anne's). Within three years they were doing so well that they built the Preissnitz Hotel.

Then a third doctor arrived, Dr E. B. Grinrod, who had his own special methods of 'medical' torture. Malvern continued to flourish, the masochists continued to arrive – helped now by the railway which had reached the town by 1861. This led to a fresh outburst of housing; great detached Victorian villas kept private by massive stone walls were built, and new roads from the station area ascended the steep hill in graceful curves to make it easier for the horse-drawn traffic.

The three doctors passed on, but the water cure endured – as did patients such as Gladstone, Florence Nightingale, Macaulay, Carlyle and Charles Darwin. Gradually a more normal spa treatment took over, as many of the rich and some of the famous set up house in Malvern. Among them was the famous soprano Jenny Lind, the 'Swedish Nightingale'. She had two cottages converted into a beautiful house just below the British Camp, the Iron Age fortress topping the Herefordshire Beacon, the second highest of the Malvern Hills.

She died there in 1891, the very year that Elgar, aged 24, returned to Malvern after a disastrous attempt to make a success in London, and one of his first major compositions was based on the British Camp. He made it the setting for *Caractacus*, the struggle of the great British prince against the Romans, even though the final battle is considered by historians to have been fought some forty miles further west. He wrote two of his greatest works, the *Enigma Variations* and *The Dream of Gerontius* at a house in Wells Road he called 'Craeg Lea', an anagram of Elgar plus E, A and C, the initials of himself, his wife and their daughter Clarice. Then the family moved to Hereford, but when they died both he and his wife were brought back for burial, and they lie in the same grave at St Wulstan's Roman Catholic Church in Wells Road, Little Malvern.

Elgar was a close personal friend of George Bernard Shaw long before the dramatist became associated with Sir Barry Jackson, founder of Birmingham Repertory Theatre, and he joined enthusiastically in the planning of the Malvern Festival, which was a national theatre event for ten years before the Second World War halted it. The first festival consisted entirely of Shaw's plays, and those which had their première with the hills as a background included *The Apple Cart* and *In Good King Charles's Golden Days*. The festival was revived in 1978.

Malvern Priory and Great Malvern which has sprung up around it

The oldest part of the priory church at Great Malvern, around which the medieval village and later the spa town grew, dates back to 1088, but there were probably monastic buildings on the site before that. The nave has the same sort of thick round pillars as Tewkesbury (although not so massive), but a major restoration in the fifteenth century gave greater light and height, and saw the installation of the three features for which the church is remarkable – its stained glass, tiles and misericords. Admirable booklets in the church go into great detail about these, but briefly the glass is more complete than any other fifteenth-century stained glass in the country and has delicate yellows and browns as well as the more conventional colours; there are about 1,200 tiles of the same period in ninety different patterns of pink, golden brown or lavender, made locally by the monks; and the twenty-four misericords include some abounding with medieval humour as well as ten of the Twelve Labours of the Year (only August and November are missing). All this would have vanished had not the villagers, only about a hundred families then, paid Henry VIII twenty pounds (in two instalments) to buy it.

Three miles south is another Norman priory church at Little Malvern, on the road back to Upton-on-Severn just after it has branched off the trunk road, the A449, from Malvern to Ledbury and Ross-on-Wye. The church consists of the space between the tower and the former choir of a twelfth-century priory, all that was allowed to remain, for parish worship, at the Dissolution. What is now used as the chancel is floored with the same kind of tiles as those at Great Malvern Priory Church, and there is most of the original rood beam. There are also ten monks' stalls, although the actual misericord seats have been hacked away, presumably by the same Parliamentary soldiers as those who left a sword in the churchyard (now in a glass case in the church) and who also seriously damaged the fifteenth-century glass in the east window. In six panels this portrayed the royal family of the time – Edward IV, his Queen Elizabeth, their two sons Edward and Richard (the little princes murdered in the Tower), their daughter Princess Elizabeth (who married Henry VII and so united the houses of York and Lancaster) and her sisters Cecily, Anne and Katherine. Now three of the lights are missing and one figure is headless.

What remains of the monastic buildings, the refectory or Prior's Hall, is now incorporated in the adjoining Little Malvern Court, a private house which is open to the public on Wednesday afternoons in the summer. The roof, dating back to the early fourteenth century, is a notable feature.

CHAPTER SEVEN

The Edge of the Saucer

The Malvern Hills are some eight miles long, with a narrow spine along their crest, but their windy slopes, close-cropped by the grazing sheep, contain more than twenty-six miles of footpaths, most of them marked by the Malvern Hills Conservators. This is a body set up by a Parliamentary Bill in 1884 to protect the common land into which the land-hungry were nibbling and quarries were gouging. They have kept up with the times, even managing to squeeze in a tolerable amount of car-parking space without spoiling the scenery.

Hardy walkers can choose any number of access points to such well-known places as St Anne's Well, Sugar Loaf Hill, the Worcestershire Beacon (the highest point of all at 1,394 feet) and the Herefordshire Beacon (1,114 feet). For the motorist, the easiest way to the first beacon is from the Wyche Cutting, which is along the B4232, a right-hand fork just out of Great Malvern driving south; for the second beacon, it is at Wynds Point, the pass through the hills on the A449, just above Little Malvern.

The Red Earl's Dyke is prominent there, as it cuts through the Iron Age fortress called British Camp which is carved so steeply and deeply into the Herefordshire Beacon that it cannot be mistaken, even from many miles away. It is a hard climb up the ramparts and down the intervening ditches to reach the topmost citadel, which is only some fifty yards across though the camp altogether covers nearly forty-five acres. A stone tablet inside the citadel records the comment by John Evelyn, the seventeenth-century diarist, that it provides 'one of the goodliest vistas in England', then adds: 'At a spring near by William Langland, the famous 14th Century poet "slombered in a sleping" and dreamt his *Vision of Piers Plowman*.'

On gazing westward, the contrast with the view to the east is so great that it could be a different country. Instead of the great flatlands of the Severn and Avon valleys leading into the Midland plain, wooded scenery delights the eye all the way to the great escarpment of the Black Mountains nearly forty miles west, forming the boundary between England and Wales.

It also provides a lesson in geology which students by the thousand come every year to study. The Hereford-shire Beacon, like the rest of the Malverns' spine to the north, is of rock the geologists call Pre-Cambrian and could be up to 1,200 million years old, according to the Institute of Geological Sciences. The Ridgeway (as it is called) starting less than a mile away, is of rock formed something over 400 million years ago, when what is called the Silurian Sea stretched across the land west-wards and lapped against the flanks of the Malverns.

At the Gullet Quarry 1¼ miles south, between Swinyard Hill and Midsummer Hill (which also has a prehistoric fort crowning it) is an example of this actually preserved in the stone. Silurian rocks containing fossils butt on to Pre-Cambrian ones through a rough-looking segment called conglomerate which was the boulder-strewn sea-beach.

The rich red earth of saucer-shaped Herefordshire, encircled by hills, was laid down in the Devonian period, which followed the Silurian and lasted for about 50 million years. Most of the wooded hills standing out in the distant lowlands are of what is called 'cornstone', because traditionally the soil from it was good for corn-growing.

Herefordshire was the last English county to be eaten out of Wales by the Anglo-Saxons – a county which has never quite accepted its forced marriage to Worcester-shire in 1974 and still claims that it is envied everywhere else for its six 'W's': Wool, Water, Wood, Wheat, Women and Wine (the latter the local cider).

From Wynds Point the B4232 runs to the Wyche Cutting, along the western slopes of the Malverns, wide open to the winds that have blown over the wooded knolls of the Herefordshire plain, to Colwall, where Elizabeth Barrett Browning lived when she was a girl with her many brothers and sisters and her father, a formidable figure in the play *The Barretts of Wimpole Street*. Now Colwall is a commuter township, partly because the mile-long railway tunnel, which must have been enor-mously hard to hack through the ancient rock, emerges at Colwall Stone, named after a huge rock probably deposited by a glacier.

Malvern water has long been bottled at Colwall from a spring with a Herefordshire Beacon source, and just north of Colwall Stone is another source, that of the Cradley Brook. This flows north through a valley cut in Silurian rocks and Mathon, which has a church with fascinating inscriptions, to Cradley village, where a fifteenth-century half-timbered building is now the parish hall. In the churchyard is a sundial with the strangely spelt words 'Thyme Tryeth Troth'.

The brook runs on through a countryside increasingly rich in hopfields and orchards to be swelled by other streams from the west and north at Batchelor's Bridge, near Suckley, the scattered village where, it is claimed, the first hop-picking machine was made. Then, as the

Leigh Brook, it winds its way among the foothills between the Malverns and riverside meadows to reach the Teme at Leigh (pronounced Lye) which has a Norman church with unusual monuments, notably to the Devereux family. The brook has twisted its way past Alfrick, with a small Norman-founded church having many panels of sixteenth- and seventeenth-century Netherlands stained-glass, and, to the south, Birch Wood, where Elgar had a small country retreat (now incorporated in a farm) where he composed most of *The Dream of Gerontius*.

Whitbourne, wedged in between the Teme and the Sapey Brook, was a manor of the bishops of Hereford in medieval times. It has more half-timbered farms and cottages than expected, many of them dating back to the years of the hunting-chase before the common land began to be enclosed at the start of the nineteenth century. And it also has a Norman church with the unusual feature of a fifteenth-century red velvet cope which probably belonged to one of the bishops of Hereford. Their moated palace near the church was enlarged by the local Parliamentary leader during the Civil War, Colonel John Birch, a colourful character who as a trader, took his goods round by packhorse. At one time he so effectively beat off some drunken Roundheads trying to rob him that Cromwell offered him a command in his troop. He rose quickly to command in Herefordshire, and captured Hereford, Leominster and Goodrich Castle for Parliament, enriching himself handsomely in the process. When peace came he developed Royalist leanings, and when he died in 1691 he had been MP for Leominster and for Weobley.

North of Whitbourne is Clifton-on-Teme, so divorced from the Teme by rising nearly six hundred feet above the river in less than a mile as the crow flies that I can never regard it as one of the valley's villages. It seems to be an outlier of Bromyard, which it must have rivalled in

The main street at Clifton-on-Teme

importance in 1270 when Henry III gave it a royal charter of borough status. Now Clifton is wreathed in its dreams, with picturesque half-timbered houses beside the huge tree on the scrap of village green and an ancient pub. The church, although heavily restored in the middle of the last century, has remains of work done in the thirteenth century, when it was built. It contains a couple of tablets said to have been carved by Grinling Gibbons.

The road through Clifton, the B4204, runs between Hanley William and Hanley Childe, imposing names but little else, to the brow at Broadheath, some 750 feet above sea level. The steady slope to the south provides the source of the Sapey Brook, which trickles away through the hamlets of Upper Sapey and Lower Sapey and below Tedstone Delamere. There the Norman church stands in a field with the remains of a deserted village, abandoned during enclosure times, humped around it. At its twin, Tedstone Wafre, a mile away on the Stourport-Bromyard road, the B4203, only the lower part of the walls of the medieval St Mary's remain.

The road gives extensive views as it runs down the spine of high land between the Sapey Brook and the Frome, the second smallest of Herefordshire's seven rivers (the others are the Wye, the Teme, the Lugg, the Arrow, the Leadon and the Lodon). Its source is also on Broadheath's slopes and it forms a valley of prolific farms flanked on its west slopes by the B4214 as the roads converge on Bromyard. Three place names within a mile seem to sum it up: Stoke Bliss, Sweet Green and Pie Corner. But only Stoke Bliss is anything more than a name on a map, with a church containing a wooden pulpit and reading desk pre-dating the Civil War.

To the south-west is Wolferlow, with ancient earthworks near its heavily restored Norman church, but there is a bigger digging on the other side of the Tenbury road, Garmsley Camp, an oval hill-fort with one wall, enclosing nine acres. These fertile hills and valleys west of the Malverns have more historic sites than is generally realized; just east of Thornbury, with a field-road running alongside it, is Wall Hills, an Iron Age hill-fort nearly three times the size of Garmsley and with much taller ramparts, up to forty feet high in places.

The roads converging on Bromyard have small settlements dotted along them, such as Bredenbury, which has a Victorian church roofed with fancy tiles, and the strangely-named 'twins', Edvin Loach and Edvin Ralph. The 'Edvin' perpetuates the name of long-dead owners, the Edefens (many of whose memorials are at Collington, on the Tenbury road). The second word in each place-name differentiates between later owners who shared the estate, the Loaches and the Ralphs.

The shopping centre for this north-east corner of Herefordshire is Bromyard, with a population of some 2,500, about the same as that of Kington. Apart from the country town (about 50,000) the other market towns are

Leominster (8,000), Ross-on-Wye (6,000), and Ledbury (4,000), so Herefordshire remains truly rural.

Bromyard, on a plateau west of the Frome, was one of the most important towns in Herefordshire long before Domesday Book. It had a Saxon church mentioned in a charter of 840, and St Peter's was probably built on the site about 1160. Two striking doorways remain from that time and there are many fourteenth-century tomb recesses both inside and out. Stored inside is a four-legged, two-handled container inscribed 'The Bromyard Bushell by Act of Parliament 1670'. This was probably formerly kept in the market hall which, until demolished in the middle of the last century, stood in the tiny Market Square, which seems almost too small to have held a building. The town was created a borough before 1300, and its street plan remains much as it was then. Half-way between Worcester and Hereford, fourteen miles from each, it became quite an important centre in coaching days, as testified to by the number of inns, notably the Falcon, whose postboys wore white hats, breeches, and yellow jackets, and the Hop Pole in the market place. Much of Bromyard's half-timbered work is obscured behind brick frontings but Tower Hill House, Rowberry House and Bible House are worth seeing.

Bromyard's famous Downs run on each side of the main Worcester road, almost linking with Bringsty Common and Badley Wood Common. They emphasize how open this area was until enclosure days . . . and they provide wonderful walking and picnic areas.

Off the Worcester road, a couple of miles out of Bromyard, a turn marked 'Brockhampton' leads to one of the National Trust's most photographed half-timbered possessions, the hall and gatehouse at Lower Brockhampton (the name does not come from 'Brock' meaning badger, but is a corruption of 'brook'). The house, dating back to the fourteenth century, provides living accommodation for the adjoining farm, but the big hall is kept open to the public, as is the fifteenth-century gatehouse spanning the moat – full of golden carp and alive with blue-green dragonflies in the summer. A moat like this was not only a protection against attack (or burglary) but kept out straying animals better than a hedge, and also provided a supply of fresh fish for meatless days. At the side of the adjacent farmyard is a ruined church, built (as are so many in the area) of tufa which is still being deposited in the middle stretches of the Sapey Brook.

The Frome Valley south of Bromyard is flanked by the B4214 to the west and the B4220 to the east. Off the latter is the hidden-away church at Stanford Bishop, which is clearly signposted. The church, reached by a rough track, stands in a round churchyard, usually a sign of Christianity taking over a pagan site, on the same principle as turning heathen feasts into religious festivals (and after all, we still use the names of pagan gods for the days of the week). Inside the church is something that may

Among the half-timbered buildings in Bromyard's main street is the Falcon Hotel (left), a noted coaching inn

pre-date the pagan Mercians – an ancient oak chair which is claimed to be the very one on which St Augustine sat during his meeting with the Celtic bishops in A.D. 603 (see Chapter 3 – Stanford Bishop also claims that the famous meeting took place within its boundaries). A pamphlet in the church tells how a Dr James Johnson rescued the chair from the house of the sexton, who had taken it home as possible firewood after it had been thrown out during the church's restoration in 1885. The doctor did extensive research, based on the chair's obvious great age and its hinges, made in a style Roman carpenters used for six centuries. He wrote a book about it and sent the chair to Canterbury Cathedral's museum, where it remained until returned in 1943.

Lanes decked with wild flowers lead on to Acton Beauchamp, with an isolated church containing an unexpected piece of Anglo-Saxon sculpture, and to the smaller of Herefordshire's two Golden Valleys (the other one, further west, is below the Black Mountains). This is where every place name seems to be Frome – Bishop's Halmond's, Castle and Canon. Bishop's Frome is the most northerly, clustered around a village green. Halmond's Frome is a hamlet with a narrow road leading to the top of Frome Hill. Castle Frome is internationally known for the font in St Michael's Church, one of the finest examples of the work of what is known as the Herefordshire school of stonemasons, which flourished from about 1140–80 with, as Pevsner puts it: 'an

accomplished art in which ruthless styling is done for a purpose'. It is carved in stone as fluidly as if it were done in wood, with complete confidence, and draws on many influences – Anglo-Saxon, Viking, French, Italian, and English Benedictine. There is nothing primitive about it, and it rivets the attention. The Castle Frome font is huge, but carved from a single block of stone, with a base of three powerful crouching animals, a short stem and a large bowl carved, appropriately for a font, with the Baptism of Christ. It remains of stunning power and originality, even after eight hundred years, and includes fishes swimming in the pool where the baptism is taking place.

Castle Frome is named after a small motte and bailey castle of which traces remain east of the church, but the real local fighting took place at the more peacefully named Canon Frome, two miles downriver. Here the moated court was regarded during the Civil War as strong enough to have a regular Royalist garrison. They gained a bad local reputation for plundering, but paid for it when in 1645 a seven-thousand-strong Scottish army, marching via Bewdley and Tenbury to attack Hereford, assaulted them in passing and, in the words of Colonel Birch, 'slew Barnard the governor and put most of the garrison (some 70) to the sword'. The Scots also damaged the court so severely that nothing dating back to those years remains. The present building, now a local authority school, dates from 1786, shown in stone above the entrance.

Brockhampton – house protected by a moat which the gatehouse (left) bridges

In its widening valley the Frome flows under a Roman road (now the A417) to be joined within half a mile by the county's smallest river, the Lodon. This, narrower than many a stream, rises ten miles north and emerges for a fleeting glimpse at Pencombe, Little Cowarne, Stoke Lacy and Much Cowarne – each a hamlet possessing a church, most of them Victorian. The 'Much' means 'big' as opposed to 'Little' and there are three other instances in Herefordshire – Much and Little Birch, Much and Little Dewchurch and Much and Little Marcle.

At Stoke Edith locally made cider and perry are available, produced at one of the three remaining small mills in the county that manage to exist in spite of the giant Bulmer's factory at Hereford (the others are at Much Marcle and Wellington).

Straddling the Frome where the Roman road to Glevum (now Gloucester) bridges it are Stretton Grandison and Ashperton, little more than hamlets although each has its church, the former with one of the best spires in Herefordshire. The link between them lies in one of those incidents in English history that comes into the 'Alfred burning the cakes' or 'Drake playing bowls' category. This Stretton perpetuates the name of the Grandisons, whose castle was at Ashperton (the site is just west of the church) and at some time in the fourteenth century it was Katherine Grandison whose garter slipped to the floor during a court dance, causing Edward III to say 'Honi soit qui mal y pense' (Shame on him who thinks evil of it), the motto of the Order of the Garter, founded in 1348 and still limited to twenty-four Knights Companions, all nominated by the Sovereign.

Four miles east, Holy Trinity at Bosbury has a tower detached from the rest of the church – a rare feature of which Herefordshire has more examples than probably any other county in England. There are nine (the others are at nearby Ledbury, Kington, Weobley, Pembridge, Garway, Holmer, Richards Castle and Yarpole) and they date from the twelfth to the fourteenth century. Nobody seems quite sure why they were detached, but the pet theory is that, built in troublous times, they were meant to act as a refuge that could be defended. Holy Trinity seems to support this theory, because all its spire's windows are narrow lancets which could be used by archers almost completely protected inside.

Unhurried Bosbury, standing on rich red earth in the middle of hopfields and orchards, has fine half-timbered houses around its churchyard, which contain the old Free Grammar School founded in 1540. The Bell is a pleasant pub, and so is the Crown, once the home of the Harfords, who have notable memorials in the parish church. The largish village, the first settlement of any size on the River Leadon, might have attained greater importance but for the competition of Ledbury (which takes its name from the same river).

Ledbury is four miles south, where roads between Tewkesbury and Hereford, Gloucester and Malvern,

Bosbury – with the parish church's detached bell-tower

made it an important junction from at least early Christian times. Now Ledbury is a major market centre. Half-timbered buildings jostle with each other, such as the Feathers in High Town; Ledbury Court, at the town's major crossing (it has been described as 'the grandest black-and-white house in the county'); and the House on Stilts, which stands on posts at the corner of New Street, into which the top storey seems to threaten to tumble.

But the immediate eye-catcher is the Market House in High Town, mounted on sixteen massive wooden pillars studded with the nail holes of centuries of billposting. Behind it is one of the most delectable streets imaginable. Small cobblestones surface traffic-free Church Lane where medieval houses cram together (although one did not arrive until 1979, when it was brought from a back-yard elsewhere in the town and re-erected, to add to the effect). Beyond the sixteenth-century offices of the local council is the Prince of Wales, an inn for at least a century before that, and the Old Grammar School, approaching its four hundredth birthday and carefully restored in 1977. It houses the Heritage Centre, staffed by volunteers most helpful with local information.

At the top of the hill, beyond two medieval church houses, stands what is regarded as the county's premier parish church, dedicated to St Michael and All Angels. There was a church on the site when Domesday Book was compiled, but the oldest parts of the present church date back to the early twelfth century. As an admirable

Ledbury's cobbled Church Lane, leading up to St Michael's

guide says, it repays leisurely study. Apart from the architectural interest (including the detached spire, 202 feet above ground at its peak), there are magnificent monuments and memorials, ranging from a thirteenth-century monk in Mass vestments to a slab commemorating the parents of Elizabeth Barrett Browning. The former is in the baptistry, where there are relics (a sword and musket balls) of the battle in Ledbury's streets in 1645 when Prince Rupert sent the Parliament forces under Colonel Massey reeling back to Gloucester. Another reminder of the same fighting can be found at the Talbot in New Street, where bullet holes are carefully preserved in the dining room.

John Masefield, former Poet Laureate, was born in Ledbury in 1878. He kept the town and the country around it alive in his works, particularly in *The Widow in Bye Street* (which is on the other side of High Town from Church Lane), *Reynard the Fox* and *The Daffodil Fields*. Daffodils flourish in the soil around here, and Eastnor Castle, an early nineteenth-century stately home a couple of miles out on the Tewkesbury road, is particularly well worth visiting in spring to see the display (the house, open to the public on specified days, has a fine collection of armour, pictures and tapestries, and the grounds have huge and rare trees). But Masefield had in mind the wild daffodils, the Lent Lilies, that before the age of the car and easy picking, made local woods and fields golden. One of the best places of all is Dymock,

where a tongue of Gloucestershire protrudes over the M50. That motorway has, in a way quite unforeseen, helped to spread the daffodils. The earth bulldozed out of Queens Wood held countless bulbs which have spread to make the central reservation between the carriageways a mass of yellow-gold in Spring.

Dymock has more than blossom to offer. It is a most picturesque village with a church going back to Anglo-Saxon times and houses in and near it which attracted a kind of residential club of poets and writers just before the First World War. The American poet Robert Frost lived at Little Iddens, at Ledington; that is half-timbered, as is the Old Nail Shop at Greenway Cross, home of Wilfred Gibson, 'the poet of the industrial poor'; Edward Thomas, whose poems included *Adlestrop* and who was killed at Arras in 1917, also lived at Ledington, at Chandlers Farm; Lascelles Abercrombie rented a thatched cottage at Ryton called The Gallows (a highwayman was hanged there); and Eleanor Farjeon, Rupert Brooke, W.H. Davies and John Drinkwater were among those who paid visits.

A couple of miles west is Kempley, a scattered hamlet which amazingly has *two* Anglican churches – one built in 1903 which contains excellent work by local craftsmen, and another, St Mary's, which goes back to early Norman times and has frescoes dating back to that time, unique in England for their completeness. They escaped the Reformation (when they were whitewashed over) and 'restoration' by the Victorians who uncovered them, and make the church's interior a glowing mass of colour.

Much Marcle, two miles north but separated by the county boundary, also has a splendid church – one of the best in Herefordshire. Outside the south porch is an enormous yew, so old that all the heart-wood has gone and inside are plank seats on which it is claimed that seven people can crowd. Inside the church is a tomb that is as much a work of art as an effigy, dated 1365 and to yet another of the Mortimers – Blanche, who married Sir Peter Grandison, lord of the manor of Much Marcle. Even more interesting is one of the few wooden memorials to survive seven centuries, representing Walter Helyon, who was seneschal (steward) to the then lord of the manor. Such survivals are so rare that it was taken to London in 1971 for an exhibition called 'Chaucer's London' at the museum in Kensington Palace, and carefully restored in what were deduced to be the original colours. Walter did well in life. He acquired the mansion of which he had been steward and which is now called 'Hellens'. It stands almost opposite the lane leading to the church and is open to visitors on Wednesday afternoons in summer – although the twelfth-century house where Walter worked was rebuilt in Jacobean times.

There is a local cider factory where the side-road into the village joins the A449, running south-west past well-treed woodland that hides Homme House, which was the home of the Kyrles but is now converted into flats. Then the main road joins the M50 just outside Ross-on-Wye, having enclosed in the angle the Norman church at Upton Bishop, where, of all things, a Roman tombstone is built into the chancel wall.

The churchyard cross, Much Marcle

CHAPTER EIGHT

Where the Welsh Hung On

Ross rises elegantly above the Wye's meander known as the Horseshoe Bend. Buildings nestling on a steep sandstone cliff reach up to the dominating spire of the parish church. They seem to have lodged themselves down the centuries on the rich red rock.

In fact, the continental-looking prospect of Ross from across the river is the result of planned building in the last 150 years. Soon after the 'picturesque medieval' became a cult, it was decided to turn Ross into a holiday town (perhaps with the success of nearby Malvern in mind). The keystone of the plan was the Royal Hotel which, opened in 1837, was where the future Queen Victoria stayed the following year. About the same time the approach road across the Wye was made to look medieval, with a round tower and town walls set with arrow-slits, all built with the local red stone. Now, with surfaces crumbling from erosion, they look to the casual eye as though they date from the Middle Ages.

Although Ross was the site of a palace for the bishops of Hereford and became a borough about 1150, it has practically no medieval history. A peaceful little market town that was one of the pioneers in the tourist industry, it owes much to one man, John Kyrle, and even he would have remained unheard of outside local confines but for the eighteenth-century poet and satirist Alexander Pope, who came to know Kyrle while on a visit to nearby Holme Lacy. He immortalized him as the Man of Ross in his *Moral Essays, The Use of Riches*.

John Kyrle was born at Dymock, a member of a family whose chapel takes up a great deal of Much Marcle church. He read law in London, but never practised, as in his twenties he inherited the then princely income of £500 a year. He settled in Ross and lavished all his love and money on the town, so that when he died in 1724, an 89-year-old bachelor, there was not a penny in his house, and not a single debt, either.

John Kyrle was best remembered for his acts of public generosity. When the spire of St Mary's was in danger of collapse, he paid for the repairs, and had it raised by forty-seven feet. He also gave the church its tenor bell –

throwing into the molten metal, at the casting, the silver tankard from which he tippled his beer or cider. He acted as a doctor to the sick, had children educated, fed the poor, started men off in business. He had a causeway built so that the town's bridge over the Wye could be reached at flood-time. He gave the town a water supply. And, perhaps his most appreciated act of all, he provided The Prospect, a walled public garden which was noted for the giant elm trees he planted there about 1700 and which were still flourishing until Dutch Elm disease killed them in the early 1970s.

Upriver from The Prospect is the bridge completed in 1960 which links the M50 with the A449 and the A40. The Wye meanders so widely that although it is fifteen miles from Ross to Hereford by road, it is thirty by boat. In the parish church the Man of Ross lies buried beneath the floor of the sanctuary, with a wall monument adjoining.

St Mary's seems broader than it is long. It is notable, too, for the great number of monuments to the Rudhall family, who for centuries were local benefactors. An alabaster statue of the last of the line, bachelor Col. William Rudhall, stands at full height, dressed – most inappropriately for a Cavalier – in Roman armour. Another feature is the east window, in which the four main lights, dating from 1430, were formerly in the Bishop's Chapel at Stretton Sugwas, just outside Hereford.

In the churchyard, at the north-east corner, the stone cross, dating back to the fourteenth century (when the Black Death hit London), has a carved inscription recording the burial of 315 people who died of another outbreak of plague three centuries later. They were buried in a pit just to the west, and that part of the churchyard has never been used since.

The Plague Cross borders on Church Street, from which the strangely named Old Maids Walk runs at the south end. But the best way back to the town centre is downhill, past the gabled, red-sandstone Rudhall Almshouses, founded in 1575. A turn down High Street leads into Ross's crowded market square, with shops clustered round the little market hall. Its upper storey is mounted on sixteen pillars, as at Ledbury – although here they are of weathered local stone. The stalls that are inside on market days overflow on to a tiny triangular space which gives a good view of the half-timbered house where John Kyrle lived. From his windows he could always see the stone medallion he had added to the market hall's south wall to show his devotion to Charles II. It bears the letters F and C intertwined in a heart, standing for 'faithful to Charles in heart'.

Kyrle's house is now divided between the local newspaper's offices and a chemist's shop, at the back of which is Kyrle's summerhouse in a tucked-away garden reached by a fern-lined climb up a narrow path. An unusual feature is the mosaic of a swan on the ground at

111

the entrance to the summerhouse – another example of Kyrle's thought for the poor. The white swan was made from the teeth of horses killed in the Civil War cavalry skirmish at Wilton Bridge leading into the town, and Kyrle paid so much a tooth to finders. The Man of Ross is also remembered in the name of one of the town's many inns. Ross is on the main road between Gloucester and Hereford, with heavy traffic problems which the spur road between the M50 and South Wales has failed to solve. The Heart of England Tourist Board has offices near the market hall, in Broad Street. There they supply details not only of other interesting buildings in the town, but about surrounding countryside, of which Woodrow Wilson, the twenty-eighth American President, wrote: 'Yesterday I rode (on horseback) for nearly 20 miles beside the Wye and of all parts of England I have seen, it has most won my heart'.

South-east of Ross is tree-clad Penyard Hill, with the main Gloucester road cutting through the attractive and aptly named village of Weston-under-Penyard. Narrow lanes snaking upwards are reminders that there were small coal-pits here – the only ones in Herefordshire – because this is the fringe of Gloucestershire's Forest of Dean. The Romans mined around here, too – but for iron. Near Bromsash, north of the trunk road, is the site of Ariconium, where excavations produced items now on display in Hereford Museum that prove this to have been a major Roman ironworks serving a wide area.

Not far away is eye-catching Bollitree Castle, where ducks swim in an ornamental moat at the roadside, against a back-cloth of red-sandstone walls, towers and battlements. The building dates back to Stuart times, but a couple of centuries ago the owner made alterations because his bride said she 'had always wanted to live in a castle'. Through the main gateway are ancient half-timbered buildings and a modern house, and to make matters even more puzzling, in the building are medieval-worked stones reputed to be from a demolished Norman castle on the other side of Weston-under-Penyard, which is a mile south.

Upriver from Ross, the Wye swings with the lanes which, sometimes running through watermeadows, now and then have to fit on narrow shelves between the river and sandstone cliffs. Big, rich farms, some with imposing houses – such as Fawley Court, where the unfenced road runs between the half-timbered building and ornamental ponds and gardens – reach into the meanders. Now Caple is at the neck of the largest of these great bends, and King's Caple is right at the point, with a bridge crossing the Wye.

At Brockhampton-by-Ross (so called to distinguish it from the one by Bromyard) is a most unusual church, built at the turn of this century; it is of local stone with a thatched roof, but concrete is used inside for important vaulting. The architect, an enthusiast of the Pre-Raphaelite Movement, designed it with medievalism in

The well-worn sandstone market hall at the heart of Ross-on-Wye

mind, and two prominently displayed tapestry angels are to Burne-Jones's designs.

Fownhope, on the Forest of Dean-Hereford road, has an old milestone by its church showing that by one road the distance to Ross is 8¼ miles and 165 yards and by another 8⅜ miles. The strung-out village, rich in half-timbering, still has its stocks and, inside the church, another splendid example of the work of the Hereford-shire carvers, a Virgin and Child with hands raised in blessing.

Insignificant Sollars Hope is one of several places claiming to be the birthplace of Dick Whittington. The third 'hope' in the area (the word means a small wooded valley) is Woolhope, the name of both the dominant hill and the tiny village at its centre, where five very minor roads converge. The Woolhope Dome, as the tumbled hill is known, is a mecca for naturalists and geologists; in 1854 the Woolhope Naturalists' Field Club, responsible for many discoveries about antiquities and natural history, was formed.

North of Fownhope, the road bridges the Wye and reaches Holme Lacy, another of the many Marcher villages named after a family that came over with the Conquest. The Scudamores, who succeeded the Lacys, left their main memorial at Holme Lacy House, claimed as the finest single house in Herefordshire. For many years it has been a hospital, and though its almost un-surpassed 1670s ceilings remain, its Grinling Gibbons wood carvings have gone, some to the Metropolitan Museum, New York.

Tombs of the Scudamores take up much of the space in Holme Lacy Church, a mile away on the Wye's west bank across the line of the former Hereford-Ross railway. Narrow lanes wind beneath the high, wooded hills of Dinedor and Aconbury, each crowned by an Iron Age camp. The lanes lead to Carey and its Cottage of Content, an ancient inn that has been extensively restored since the mid-1970s when a couple leaving Rhodesia, now Zimbabwe, settled there. Since then other families have made the area something of a haven for white Rhodesians.

A road squeezed in between river and cliff leads to Hoarwithy, a popular holiday spot, with a church even more unusual than nearby Brockhampton's. At the top of a steep flight of steps is a building that seems straight from Southern Italy, campanile and all. The nave has been embellished with Byzantine effects, in-cluding gold mosaics and lapis lazuli – all because the clergyman who was Hoarwithy's vicar for more than half a century lavished his personal fortune on his church, even importing Italian workmen. St Catherine's is so unusual that it has been prey to vandals; the key has to be obtained from the vicarage, which adjoins the church.

The village's unusual name means the whitebeam, the downy-leafed red-berried shrubby tree which must have been abundant locally. It comes from the Anglo-Saxon, as do the names of other little hamlets hereabouts, Bolstone and Ballingham. But the names Much and Little Dewchurch, signposted at Hoarwithy's centre, come from quite a different culture although the names seem so basically English.

This south-west quarter of Herefordshire remained Welsh longer than anywhere else. 'Dewchurch' means 'church of St Dewi' – Welsh for St David. Nearby Sellack is also from the same language, and means 'church of St Suluc' – a pet-name for St Tysilio, to whom Sellack church (Norman with fine Jacobean woodwork) is dedicated.

It is a dedication unique in England, and there are other unusual dedications in the area enclosed between the Wye, the Monnow and Offa's Dyke – something like 250 square miles in all. Most of this was an independent Welsh state within England for something like six centuries until well after the Norman Conquest. It was called Archenfield and its warriors had the doubtful honour, under the Anglo-Saxons, of leading the army in attack and holding the rear in retreat.

Archenfield has possibly the longest history of uninterrupted Christianity in the country, going back to Roman times. It produced Dubricius, a major religious figure in the sixth century. A member of a Welsh royal family, he founded a community of monks at Hentland, instructing something like two thousand there before moving to Moccas, on the south bank of the Wye near Madley. He became the first Bishop of Llandaff and died on Bardsey Island, off the Lleyn Peninsula in North Wales.

Thirteen hundred years later, his name still lives in Archenfield, a sparsely populated countryside with scarcely even a village of any size, but with more than fifty parish churches, many sites of motte and bailey castles and enduring traditional houses. Its layout is another of the clues which remain of Archenfield. It reflects the age-old Celtic way in which farmsteads would be dispersed around a church but with no central settlement. And the noticeably small fields, producing anything that will scratch a living on the steep little hillsides, are relics of the old Welsh system by which a farm would be divided between a man's sons on his death. It might have seemed fair when it started but it had to be abandoned when farms became split into too tiny units.

Perhaps the easiest viewpoint from which to understand Archenfield is from the Hereford-Ross road, with the countryside laid out like a huge map westwards to the scarp of the Black Mountains twenty miles away. St Dubricius's Hentland (the name is Welsh, 'hen llan', meaning the old church) is on the east side of that road, about four miles out of Ross, with a couple of houses adjoining the Victorian-restored church which could well stand on the site of the sixth-century monastery. It

115

takes some finding, as do many in this little-explored corner of the county, which has three more churches dedicated to Dubricius and one each to other Celtic holy men: Deinst, Dinebo and Weonard (the fourth unique dedication was back at Sellack).

Meandering on from Ross, the Wye runs alongside the A40, then below the wooded slopes that half-conceal Goodrich Castle to slip under Kerne Bridge, well known by anglers because nearby was the home of one of the most famous salmon fishermen of all time, Robert Pashley, who died in 1956. It is a longish walk to the castle from Goodrich village, but a most rewarding one, with the red-sandstone walls suddenly rising from identical bedrock in the middle of a dry moat. The satirist Dean Swift's grandfather was vicar of Goodrich during the Civil War and, as a staunch Royalist, had the silver chalice looted. His grandson recovered it some seventy-five years later and gave it back to the parish. Wordsworth also had Goodrich connections, and wrote his famous *We Are Seven* as the result of a visit; he was 50 when Goodrich Court, which he called an 'impertinence' was built in 1830, and although it has been pulled down and exported to the United States, the village hostelry, of the same period and style, still remains.

The Wye's meanders become outrageous downstream of Goodrich, sweeping down to isolated Welsh Bicknor, where it becomes the county boundary with Gloucestershire. Then, at Symonds Yat, the Wye is forced by the hard rock of Huntsman Hill to make a five-mile loop before coming back only a few hundred yards from where it began. A small vantage-point on top of the Yat Rock, walled to give a sense of security to those peering down the precipitous limestone cliffs to the Wye coiling below, encloses a Victorian relief map which indicates and names the various hills, such as the Great and Little Doward, crowned by a hill-fort, a well and tumuli, and the Seven Sisters Rocks, where a footpath passes King Arthur's Cave, which dates back at least eight thousand years to the Middle Stone Age – the oldest trace of man in Herefordshire.

Symonds Yat is approached from the A40 by a small motorway-style junction at Whitchurch, the most southerly village in this part of Herefordshire, with its church dedicated to St Dubricius. The border with Wales is a couple of miles away, and just as the outlying houses of Monmouth are about to come into sight, there is a minor road signposted to Ganarew, which has a Victorian church and just a couple of houses. Out of the Wye Valley the land becomes hillier and Welsh place-names predominate. On the east of the Monmouth-Hereford road, almost in a straight line pointing northwards, are Llangrove and Llangarron, Tretire and Pencoyd. Each is a hamlet with a church, Llangarron's being dedicated to St Dinebo. Llanwarne has two churches, one of them in ruins.

On the Welsh boundary are Welsh Newton and St

Weonard's, the latter named after its church. They are linked through a priest, John Kemble, who was born at St Weonard's and whose tomb-slab is under the cross in Welsh Newton churchyard. In 1679, at the age of 80, he was executed for being a Jesuit. He was canonized in 1970 and one of his hands is kept as a relic at St Francis Xavier's R.C. Church in Hereford.

From Welsh Newton twisty, hilly lanes run along the hillside looking down on the Monnow which drains the Black Mountains and forms the Welsh boundary for many miles. The lanes lead to Garway, which eight hundred years ago was an estate of the Knights Templar. They were a military order formed to protect pilgrims to the Holy Land but they became so rich and powerful that they had to be suppressed in 1312. They liked to build churches with round naves as in the Temple at Jerusalem, and traces of this in St Michael's account for its odd appearance.

Upriver the great deer park of Kentchurch Court fills the northern horizon. One of Owen Glendower's three daughters became its Lady, by marriage. Two miles north is Pontrilas, which before Sunday licensing in Wales was a haven for thirsty Welshmen.

Joining on to the Monnow River is the Worm Brook which wriggles secretively through rich arable land and wooded hills. Near the source is Much Dewchurch, the church of which is crammed with memorials to Pyes and Symonses, between them owners of the parish's big estate, The Mynde, since Elizabethan times.

Norman arch into the chancel of the Knights Templar church at Garway

The most famous parish church in the area, though, is at Kilpeck, on the A465 about eight miles out of Hereford. A twisting lane, crossing railway line and brook, leads to what is probably the best-preserved church of its kind in the country. The masons who worked on it used a local red sandstone amazingly resistant to erosion. Where it was quarried no-one knows, but it has withstood the effects of rain and snow, frost and wind, since the middle of the twelfth century. The quirks of fancy of the stone-carvers of the Herefordshire School audaciously mingled paganism and naturism with piety, and the detail

South side of the elaborately carved church at Kilpeck

remains crisp and clear. To be given full justice, Kilpeck's carvings need a detailed guidebook, binoculars and plenty of time. But with even the most casual inspection the sensual detail in the south doorway and the slightly more ponderous strength of the saints of the chancel arch impresses.

Yet perhaps most enthralling of all are the corbels – blocks of stone protruding from walls and often assembled by Norman builders into a corbel table below the roof eaves. The blank spaces provided masons with chances to show their skills, and those of Kilpeck are carved with wry impishness. Rabbits and songbirds jostle with a contorted crocodile and an elephant, a muzzled bear with a mermaid combing her hair, the Lamb of God with a sheila-na-gig (an obscenely presented female figure generally supposed to be either a fertility figure or a warning against lechery). That this last should survive a tactful restoration in 1848 that left other Kilpeck corbels blank (about eighty survive) leads one to wonder what those were like.

Kilpeck is an old Archenfield site (Saxon work survives in the nave's north-east wall) but a Norman developed it. Within a mile of Kilpeck are two other Norman churches at St Devereux (a corruption of Dubricius) and The Worm's only other settlement, Wormbridge.

Just north of Pontrilas is Ewyas Harold, chosen by a Norman for its strategic value. The first word (pro-nounced e-wyas, with the accent on the last-but-one syllable) is Welsh and means 'sheep district'; the word 'ewe' survives. The second is that of the second Norman Earl of Hereford, and not that of Harold slain at Hastings (although he led a major punitive campaign against the Welsh in this area in 1063, three years before Edward the Confessor died).

Ewyas Harold is one of the three places in Herefordshire (the others are Hereford and Richard's Castle, in the north) where a Norman built a castle well before the Conquest. All that remains of the castle, once one of the most vital frontier posts in the Marches, is the tump that was the motte, in hummocky ground on a tongue of land overlooking the village centre from the other side of the Dulas Brook. The little central oblong of lanes and the size of the church are all that is left to indicate that in Domesday times this was one of the only five boroughs in Herefordshire.

North of the village the B4347 leads into the county's larger and better-known Golden Valley. Its dozen miles are rich and peaceful now. At harvest time the name seems astonishingly apt, but it is most probably a Norman confusion between the French *d'or*, meaning golden, and the Welsh *dwr*, meaning water. At the southern end are the remains of the chief treasure, Abbey Dore, a huge twelfth-century Cistercian abbey. This order of monks specialized in producing wool – some of the finest in the country. In 1535, the site and buildings passed to a Scudamore of Holme Lacy, whose great-

great-grandson, the first Viscount Scudamore, had the ruins turned into the present church some hundred years later. Pevsner describes it as 'odd-looking' and it certainly is much too high for its surface area. But from inside the way in which the arches surge skywards is awe-inspiring.

The Romans knew this site; their road from South Wales to the regional capital of Kenchester, west of Hereford, lies under the goods yard of Abbey Dore station, extinct itself since 1957 when the Golden Valley Railway closed. The road up-valley passes close enough to the hamlet of Bacton for a look at an isolated church closely linked with the political intrigues of Tudor times. Bacton Church contains the tomb of Blanche Parry, who returned to this quiet countryside after a lifetime devoted to Queen Elizabeth I which included a spell in the Tower of London with her. A long inscription, quaintly spelt (such as 'in pryncys courte wythe gorgious wyghts') ends with the often-quoted line 'Wythe maeden quene a maede dyd ende my lyffe'. In a frame on the north wall hangs embroidery attributed to Blanche Parry.

Vowchurch and the even tinier Turnastone straddle the Dore halfway up the valley, their churches a stone's throw apart on either bank. They have Norman remains and timber roofs worth seeing. This is where a gap in the hills gives access to the valley from the Wye plain to the east, and a small bridge leads to the hilly valleys to the west. Warriors of long ago saw the strategic importance.

The church at Ewyas Harold, one of Herefordshire's five boroughs in Domesday Book

On the western slopes are the remains of ruined Norman castles – below St Margaret's (where the lonely church has one of the finest rood screens in the Marches), and at Urishay and Snodhill. Midway between Vowchurch and Peterchurch (the valley's biggest village), the slopes east of the road and river are the site of a British fort, excavated between the two World Wars, which was possibly last strengthened to oppose the Romans.

Peterchurch houses the Golden Valley's comprehensive school, the biggest collection of shops and inns, and a church on a site that St Peter himself is supposed to have visited. According to an old legend, he consecrated the well near the church and to mark this, dropped in a carp with a golden chain round its neck. A tablet inside the church commemorates this, and in confirmation that St Peter came here (supposedly with St Paul, blown off course while on a missionary voyage to Spain) locals point out that the north wall of the Black Mountains is crossed by Bwlch Efengeli, which is Welsh for the Pass of the Evangelists, or Gospel Pass. The parish church itself has four segments, one more than normal. The extra segment could well be the base of a long-vanished tower. If so, St Peter's is unlucky with its towers; the present spire is of plastic, set there in the mid-1970s to replace one centuries older that had fallen.

At the head of the valley, ringed by hills which the road to Hay crosses at Scotland Bank, is Dorstone, a typical 'planted' village, with castle mound, a tiny triangular

The abbey remains at Abbey Dore, seen through the lych gate

121

Arthur's Stone, high on the hills at the head of the Golden Valley

years ago, it was covered with earth or turfs but this has vanished, and the stones now stand bare. The site, in the care of the Department of the Environment, is reached by a track off the lane from Dorstone to Bredwardine in the Wye Valley below, which crosses the ridge with gradients of one-in-four on each side.

The wildest and least explored part of Herefordshire is the seventy-square-mile rectangle between the Golden Valley and Offa's Dyke as it runs along the crest of the Black Mountains escarpment. This was where for many centuries the Welsh battled against invaders from the east. Here the River Monnow and two tributaries cut deep into the rock, and in a loop of the Monnow is the tiny hamlet of Rowlstone with a church that has one of the finest Herefordshire School carvings, of a Christ in Glory. North lies Longtown, with a round Norman keep overlooking the Monnow that was restored in the late 1970s. This was the place that the powerful de Lacys set up in their attempts to dominate the local Welsh, as the village's former name of Ewyas Lacy testifies, and it was probably from here that in 1193 Hugh de Lacy rode westward over the escarpment to found Llanthony Abbey in the Vale of Ewyas.

Another motte and bailey stands on the other side of the village near the hamlet of Clodock, which has a watermill and a Norman church with the only dedication in the world to St Clodock, the anglicized name of a king and martyr killed while hunting in A.D. 540.

market place and a Norman church. This has connections with Richard de Brito, one of the four knights who murdered Archbishop Thomas Becket in Canterbury Cathedral and who settled in Dorstone after completing fifteen years of exile in Palestine. The village takes its name from the river and the prehistoric burial chamber a mile north-east on Merbach Hill. It is called Arthur's Stone and it consists of a huge slab of sandstone twenty feet long balanced on vertical stones and approached by a narrow entrance. When it was built about five thousand

North of Longtown a lane to the north-east leads to the Escley Brook and Michaelchurch Escley, where the church's north wall has a medieval wall-painting of a rare subject known as the Christ of the Trades – Jesus surrounded by tools such as shears, adze and flail. It was supposed to warn people that those who worked on the Sabbath kept open the wounds of Christ.

On the Olchon Brook is Llanveynoe with two crudely carved slabs of stone that may be Saxon in the church. The Monnow runs from Craswell, where its source lies under Hay Bluff, towering well over a thousand feet above the hamlet. A mile beyond the narrow bridge over the infant river is a farm-road marked 'Abbey', towards the end of which lie the few remains of one of the only three priories of the Order of Grandmont in the country. Just a little further on, the road, a rough track until recent years, reaches its peak at Parc y Meirch, where the Ordnance Survey map gives the height as approximately 1,450 feet. The views lose little as the road plunges down the steep wooded cleft in the Black Mountains' north face that is called Cusop Dingle. Cusop village, to all intents and purposes a suburb of Hay nowadays, has traces of a Norman castle near the church, which is of the same period, with yews in the churchyard supposed to be the ones mentioned in Domesday Book. There is also what is known as the Martyr's Grave, burial place of William Seward, a disciple of John Wesley, who was stoned to death by a mob in 1791.

Although local people prefer not to discuss it, Cusop is also the place where the infamous poisoner Major Herbert Armstrong lived while practising law at Hay. He murdered his wife and later sent a box of poisoned chocolates to a fellow solicitor. His wife's body was exhumed and he was found guilty of murder and hanged. His waxwork found a place in the Chamber of Horrors at Madame Tussauds, but his house still stands in Cusop. Little wonder that its name has been changed.

CHAPTER NINE

The Wye Starts Meandering

The Wye, born on Plynlimon's slopes near the source of its big sister, the Severn, has lost its youthful vigour by the time it has turned east by the great bulk of the Black Mountains and is flowing through fertile level land as it enters England at Hay. Offa's Dyke crosses it almost at right angles at what were the railway sidings of this seemingly much more English than Welsh historic little market town in Powys.

Hay, near the tip of a salient pointing into Wales that the Romans knew, had a Norman castle soon after the Conquest (the motte is near the parish church), but it must have been abandoned within a century, because the main castle dominating the town centre was built at the beginning of the thirteenth century. In almost constant border warfare Hay was burned five times, and the second castle never recovered militarily from the Glendower uprising of 1402. Fire continued to plague it after it became a private house and caused severe damage in 1977.

What is left looks down on Market Street, where a disproportionate number of shops (and the former cinema) sell second-hand books – Hay claims to have the biggest concentration of used books for sale in Britain. Market Street also has two small halls opulently built of stone, the Cheese Market and the Butter Market, dating from the 1830s. The former is on two floors and the latter, single-storeyed, is distinguished by small columns around it. Beyond the Butter Market is the square known as the Bull Ring. At the foot of the little shopping area running down from Market Street is the town clock, housed in a two-storey obelisk so obviously Victorian that it scarcely needs to have the date of 1881 on it.

From the clock tower, Bridge Street leads to the two alternative roads to Hereford, the B4351 crossing a new bridge to pick up the main Brecon-Hereford 'A' road, and the B4348 using the Wye's south bank through the historic village of Clifford and then providing access to the old toll bridge over the river near Whitney. This, on its great wooden pillars, may look frail by modern standards but it provides an impressive view of the Wye

The Victorian clock-tower at Hay-on-Wye

flowing in slow maturity. The old toll-house has a board with an interesting scale of charges ranging from laden farm carts to lambs, and cows to pedal cycles.

Clifford is named after a great Norman family best remembered for the Jane Clifford known as Rosa Munda – the Rose of the World – who became the mistress of Henry II. The Clifford stronghold was never restored after Glendower's war but the strength of the castle was such that much of the great keep and five of the towers still stand, 150 feet above the river. Clifford was such a strategic site that there are two other castles in the parish, at Castletown and Newton Tump; the three form a triangle with sides about two miles long. Clifford was an enormous parish, and there is an old jingle which runs: 'Clifford, Clyro, Clodock and Clun are the largest parishes under the Sun'. Did it come before or after Housman's famous doggerel couplet about the four villages in the Clun Valley in Shropshire? Clifford Church at the head of a steep lane is notable for the old wooden effigy of a priest which experts date at about 1280 – the only other one in Herefordshire being on the other side of the county at Much Marcle.

A great river-loop is crossed by the B4348 on the way to Bredwardine, the next village down valley to have a bridge. The unusual ending 'wardine' is confined to the Welsh Marches, with Herefordshire and Shropshire having more than any other county, perhaps forty in all; it means a settlement on a hillside. Bredwardine has

125

Bredwardine Churchyard. Kilvert's grave is left of the great yew tree

probably become the best-known of all since it is here that the Rev. Francis Kilvert, author of the famous diaries, is buried. His writings give a unique picture of life in Victorian England. He became vicar of Bredwardine in November 1877, and died of peritonitis in September 1879, only ten days after returning from his honeymoon. The Kilvert Society have put a seat at the entrance to the churchyard beneath the great yew which he must have known well. His white-marble tombstone on the north side of the churchyard stands out because it gleams with care, whereas the only other two marble crosses there are dulled with age. Kilvert's wife, who survived him by thirty-one years, could not be buried beside him because there was not enough room. She is buried in the new cemetery several hundred yards away, with a similar white marble cross. The village's Norman church contains two tombs, of which one is supposed to be of a lord of the manor who was killed defending Henry V at Agincourt. As well as a famous fishing pub the village has a six-arched brick bridge which crosses the Wye at a spot where the cliffs seem to provide plenty of protection against flooding, but there are times when the Wye, swollen by melting snow, can rise more than twenty feet with little warning. The Old Toll House, now a private dwelling, is on record as having been nearly covered. On a fine day the view from the bridge is breathtaking, especially downstream to Moccas Court.

At Moccas, we are back in St Dubricius country. He is supposed to have moved his college of priests from Hentland to a site near Madley, where he was born, choosing it because he saw a white sow with a litter of piglets; hence the name Moccas, which is Welsh for a damp meadow where pigs live. Moccas now consists of a few houses outside the grounds of Moccas Court, which also contain the small church of St Michael. Pevsner says this would be the perfect example of a Norman village church but for a bellcote and some Decorated windows which had to be inserted to admit extra light. The present court, which is open to the public, dates from the last thirty years of the eighteenth century, but is on a much older site. For three hundred years it was the home of the Cornewalls, one of the most famous Herefordshire families, but the last of them, Sir Jeffrey, who was a bachelor, moved into a small house in the grounds in 1916 and thirty years later sold all the contents and furniture and leased the property. Consequently it is not so fully furnished as might be expected, but the present owner, a distant relative of the Cornewalls, is rebuilding the collection. The most striking feature of the house is a magnificent circular room which overlooks the Wye. Its walls are covered with French wallpaper nearly two hundred years old and no fires have ever been allowed in the room for fear of damaging this. It also has a cunningly concealed doorway in the circular walls. One of the recently discovered features of the grounds, which were laid out by

Windmill converted into a private house near Moccas in the Wye Valley

'Capability' Brown, is a fern garden along the banks of a tiny stream trickling down to the river.

Twisting lanes converge on Madley, a tiny village with a parish church that is exceptionally large because of thirteenth-century pilgrimages. Glass from around this period remains in the east window and the font is claimed to be the second largest in England. Beyond the village store is a small group of modern houses with a name-plate showing that they stand in Pennyplock and Rosemary Lane.

St Mary's at Tiberton has a remarkable eighteenth-century reredos, but practically every other church in the Madley area is medieval. That at Eaton Bishop has in its east window perhaps the finest fourteenth-century stained glass in the county. Commemorated in the window is the abbot who gave it to the church in 1328.

In spite of modern housing Clehonger remains a separate village entity, and just two miles from Hereford is the Benedictine house of Belmont Abbey, which took nearly thirty years to build in Victorian times. After being a cathedral for more than sixty years until 1920, it is now an abbey with an independent Roman Catholic school attached and is open to visitors every day.

The faster road from Hay to Hereford entails leaving Hay by the concrete bridge built in 1959 on the site of the old railway bridge that carried the Hereford-Hay-Brecon line. Within a mile it reaches Clyro where Kilvert was curate for seven years and where he wrote many of his best anecdotes, including some featured in the BBC television series about his diaries. The parish church built in 1850 is as he knew it; Ashbrook House, where he lodged during part of his curacy, is still there; and so is Clyro Court, mentioned so often in his writing, which now, though, is an hotel. Conan Doyle stayed at the court while researching for his famous Sherlock Holmes story, *The Hound of the Baskervilles*. He was connected by marriage to the Baskervilles, as was the fifteenth-century Black Vaughan, who was reputed to have become a great black hound haunting the Welsh Marches. His tomb is at Kington, a few miles north.

Where the widened A438 (which follows the line of the old Roman road between Brecon and Hereford) crosses into England is the Rhydspence Inn, a half-timbered building much more impressive than it seems from the road because, having cut the corner, the old front door is now at the back! It is in the parish of Brilley, which rises 800 feet from the river banks to rough hill grazing. The National Trust owns Cymmau Farmhouse, a seventeenth-century homestead still worked near the top of the highest hill (apart from bank holidays, it is open only by appointment).

The huge house to the north of the A438 is Whitney Court, built at the turn of the last century, and almost opposite is the Boat Inn, which provides a splendid view from the lounge almost overhanging the Wye. In 1720 floods swept away much of Whitney Church. In the same stretch of flood plain, Winforton straddles the road with black-and-white houses, and Willersley also straggling along, has so lost importance that its parish church has been converted into a private house.

At the junction eastwards, the Hereford-Kington road leads to Eardisley, high on the hills that separate the valleys of the Wye and the much smaller Arrow. It is a large village by Herefordshire standards (about six hundred inhabitants) and has a long main street crossing two streams. Half-timbered, brick and stone buildings exist happily together with a largish Norman church notable for its font, at the Wye end of the village. Pevsner ranks the font as equalling Castle Frome's in excellence. It is another Herefordshire Carvers' delight, smacking a great deal of the work at Kilpeck. The subject this time is the Harrowing of Hell, the story of what Christ did when he descended into Hell, defeated Satan and brought out Adam; this example even has a tiny man representing Adam. At the other end of the village is the Tram Inn, the name of which is a reminder that Eardisley was the terminus of the tram line from Hay, used by horse-drawn vehicles. The lane at the side of the inn leads to the Great Oak, which was mentioned in Domesday Book and also in a fifteenth-century document. The tree, standing near a small chapel, is hollow inside with holes plugged with concrete, and is big enough to shelter half-a-dozen people.

In the lanes to the north-east are Alneley, with an

129

The Rhydspence Inn, for many years the first pub in England for thirsty Welshmen

unusual painted ceiling in the parish church, and Alneley Wooton, where a seventeenth-century meeting house has belonged to the Society of Friends since 1675. The Quakers were strong in Herefordshire three hundred years ago and this quiet hamlet was as important to them then as Hereford, Leominster and Ross.

At Kinnersley, on the way back to the Wye Valley, the church, in front of a converted castle, has a curiously high fourteenth-century tower. Still nearer the Wye is a stretch of flat land known as Letton Lake – a constant reminder of the Ice Age hereabouts as it is still flooded in some winters. The effects of the Wye Valley glacier can be seen all the way to Hereford, in the hummocky hills and hollows which have resulted from the deposits of gravel and boulder clay. Letton church door, with iron nails and strap-hinges, is estimated to be about eight hundred years old.

Staunton-on-Wye, the next village down valley, lies north of the old Roman road, on what once was common land. Many of its varied houses were built by squatters of centuries ago, and their presence is corroborated by such names as World's End and Little London, reached by Duck Street and Pig Street.

The Wye's extravagant loops take it near the main road in some places and more than a mile away in others. As a result there are only scattered houses and the villages of Monnington-on-Wye and Bridge Sollars on the north bank in the last few miles into Hereford. At the former village, a broken slab outside the church door is supposed to mark the grave of Owen Glendower; the latter provides what its name suggests – another crossing of the Wye. Nearby is The Weir, a National Trust property, perched on a 50-foot cliff above the Wye and notable for the splendour of its gardens in spring.

North of the Roman road, the wooded hills rise steeply and are of the same geological formation as those fringing the Black Mountains and the Golden Valley. They are cornstone, and provide hard rocks which have been extensively quarried for roads and buildings.

Mansell Gamage shows in its disused church how these rocks have withstood the centuries. Its twin, Mansell Lacy, is one of the most charming villages in Herefordshire, with a wealth of old half-timbered buildings, notably a former post office with a 300-year-old dovecote in its roof.

Yazor Church, a mile west, commemorates a remarkable man, Sir Uvedale Price. It was built in his memory by his son, also named Uvedale, in Early English style in the mid-nineteenth century when the Price family lived at and owned Foxley – an early-eighteenth-century brick mansion in the valley below just east. The father was perhaps the most important of the instigators of the English Picturesque movement, which developed a new style of laying out the gardens and grounds around stately homes. He considered that 'Capability' Brown

The unusual tower of Kinnersley Church

had made such planned layouts too mellow, and so tried to avoid 'taming' the landscape. He emphasized natural features instead. Foxley has gone completely now but in the grounds remain some of the plantings he made.

Sir Uvedale's chief companions in the Picturesque movement were Richard Payne Knight and Thomas Andrew Knight, brothers who were born a mile from Foxley over the top of Yarsop Hill, at Wormsley Grange. Both became national figures, and Richard built perhaps the most outstanding of all Picturesque houses, at Downton Castle, near Ludlow. Their tombchests stand side by side at Wormsley's abandoned parish church.

The wooded hills around Wormsley were once probably one great plateau protected from erosion by a thin sheet of limestone, but time has broken them up into different hills which at close range seem steep and high, and dominate the landscape, yet they look almost like little green button mushrooms from the far-away Malverns. They stud the landscape all the way to Hereford – Merry Hill, Nupton Hill, Credenhill, Burghill. All contain excellent building stone which comes in greys and greens as well as reds, with the bands sometimes very close together so that, as at Wormsley church, buildings containing them look like dully coloured layer-cake.

The main road to Hereford traverses the Roman city of Magnis (later Kenchester) using deep-cut lanes through Bishopstone, where the church organ once belonged to Eton College. Two other examples of the skill of the Herefordshire Carvers are at Brinsop and Stretton Sugwas. The former is of St George on horseback piercing the dragon with his lance, the latter of Samson astride a limp-legged lion, tearing its jaws apart.

Hereford, two-thirds the size of Worcester, has at its heart a fifty-acre site which was developed in the Dark Ages after Roman Kenchester had been abandoned. King Offa, of the famous dyke, played a major part in this, and also left Hereford with a Christian martyr. When Ethelbert, an East Anglian King, wanted to marry Offa's daughter, he was murdered, possibly with the idea that Offa would govern two kingdoms that way. Later Ethelbert was canonized, and Hereford Cathedral is still dedicated to him, and the Virgin Mary.

The name 'Hereford' is Old English for 'army ford' – and Harold Godwinson, later King of England for a few frantic months, probably crossed the Wye here, near the old bridge, in punitive expeditions against the Welsh ordered by Edward the Confessor. When Harold died at Hastings the Normans quickly appreciated Hereford's strong position for holding back the Welsh. All the early kings visited the city, which was a frontier stronghold, a bishop's see and a prosperous market town. Its trade received a bitter blow from Henry VIII, who ordered its fulling mills to be destroyed, and it had a bad time during the Civil War, when its Royalist garrison first withstood a month-long siege by a Scottish army, and then fell to a surprise attack by the redoubtable Colonel Birch.

The city's siting on low-lying ground, hemmed in between the Wye and the mile-long semicircle of the town walls, was causing drainage and health problems by the middle of the eighteenth century. There were business interests too, so the walls, with their five gates and fifteen bastions, were pulled down to make trading easier. Coincidentally, in 1786, the great west tower of the cathedral collapsed, causing great damage to the fabric, and as more demolition went on and more buildings and streets vanished, Hereford began to lose its medieval look. Now, from High Town, the city's main shopping area, only two of the half-timbered buildings for which the county is famous, and two church spires, remain to represent Tudor times and earlier.

The spire to the west, that of All Saints, has a noticeable kink. When it was added in the fourteenth century to an earlier tower, everything took an alarming tilt to the north because the tower had been built on an old ditch. Restorers in the early nineteenth century decided to rebuild the top section of the spire so that it was as vertical as possible. All Saints is almost entirely medieval within, its chief treasure being its library of chained books. There are some three hundred of these – the largest collection in any parish church in the country.

The church to the east of High Town is St Peter's, the city's civic church. It has excellent Early English work inside but is mostly notable for the fact that from its battlements, in 1085, the Norman lord Walter de Lacy,

who had been granted large estates in the Marches, fell to his death while inspecting the building work.

The half-timbered building at the St Peter's end of High Town is The Old House, the sole survivor of what was Butchers' Row. Hereford is lucky to retain it, because in the 1860s there were those who wanted it to go, too, 'in the interests of the improvement and salubrity of the city'. Built in 1621, it is now a museum furnished with items from all parts of Herefordshire, including a 400-year-old yew dining table. Upstairs, as well as a magnificent wooden overmantel, are items to do with Hereford's famous actors – the Kembles; Sarah Siddons, who was a Kemble until she married another actor; and David Garrick, who was baptized at All Saints in 1717. The only other medieval building in sight is the front of a half-timbered shop – preserved by the expedient of being hoisted above ground level and used as an eye-catcher in the first and second storeys of a multiple store!

Between the two half-timbered buildings is Church Street, the most picturesque of the many approaches to the cathedral. It is by no means large as cathedrals go, and has been much restored, but there are treasures inside. The work of the Norman builders is best studied in detail from the guides inside, but for those not architecturally minded, a climb up a spiral stone staircase to the library should not be missed. It contains the largest collection of ancient chained books in the world, with

Hereford Cathedral, seen over the medieval Wye Bridge from the modern Greyfriars Bridge

something like 1,500 volumes. Many of these are hand-written, the earliest of all dating back to the seventh century, and there are also two printed by Caxton.

On the other side of the cathedral is the Mappa Mundi, drawn about 1300 by a monk and showing the world as it was then thought to be – flat and round. Jerusalem is at the centre of the world and England at the top left, while the continents and oceans are peopled by strange beings and plants. Among the tombs is one to Bishop Mayew, who was sent by Henry VII in 1501 to escort Catherine of Aragon back as the bride of Prince Arthur.

East of the cathedral is Castle Green, surrounded by elegant Georgian and Victorian houses (many of them now offices). It was here that Hereford Castle stood from before the Conquest, but now not a stone of it remains in sight, although by searching, remains of the Watergate can be found on the river bank. The sixty-foot column in the middle of the lawns is to Horatio Nelson, but there is an urn on top instead of a statue of the famous admiral; funds ran out before the work was completed in 1809.

Just upriver of the cathedral is the old Wye Bridge, which can be approached by a narrow lane past the bishop's palace, with a wall plaque marking the birth-place of Nell Gwynn, Charles II's much-loved orange-seller who became a Drury Lane actress. The fifteenth-century bridge, of six arches spanning nearly 250 feet, was augmented in 1969 by the Greyfriars Bridge a couple of hundred yards upstream.

The new bridge is an integral part of Hereford's relief road, the route of which, it was found while work was in progress, follows the line of the long-lost town walls, and unsuspected sections of walls made from earth, wood and stone were revealed.

Outside these, in Widemarsh Street, an almshouse was established in 1614 for 'worn-out soldiers, sailors, and servants' by one of the Conyngsbys – it is said that Nell Gwynn told Charles II about it, and that led to the establishment of the Chelsea Pensioners. Now the Conyngsby Hospital is a museum, with a tall stone cross in the well-kept grounds. Until the Reformation Dominican monks preached from it and it is astonishing that it escaped destruction. Now it is probably the best surviving cross of its kind in the country.

Hereford has several other museums. The main one is the public library museum in Broad Street, at the west end of the cathedral. It has exhibits from all parts of Herefordshire going back to pre-Roman times, but perhaps the city's best-known museum nationally is the Bulmer Railway Centre near Hereford railway station. Part of it is inside the premises of the huge cider-making company, so the museum is open to the general public only at weekends. The steam engines there include the Great Western's King George V and the L.M.S. Princess Elizabeth, and among the rolling stock is a coach called 'Aquila', which was made for Queen Victoria as part of her royal train and was used by succeeding monarchs. It still has the original furniture including triangular hide-covered seats at the corners of the coach. Some weekends the engines are in steam, and enquiries about when this will be should be made to the local office of the Heart of England Tourist Board. The same applies to the Herefordshire Waterworks Museum, at Broomy Hill, not far from Greyfriars Bridge. This is open on Sunday afternoons in summer, and also has an annual working day for its two rare steam-pumping engines.

Hereford's other museum is at Churchill Gardens, on Aylstone Hill, near the city boundary and just off the main road to Worcester. There are displays of furniture, paintings and costume – and Roaring Meg, probably the most formidable single weapon ever used in Herefordshire's many centuries of warfare. A huge, stumpy cannon-cum-mortar, the 200-lb cannon balls she lobbed out demolished the strongest defences, notably at Goodrich Castle, during the Civil War. She seems forlorn, out in the suburbs, after many years at the heart of Hereford, on Castle Green.

CHAPTER TEN

Half-timbered Heritage

Three miles east of Hereford a long, narrow stone bridge leads into Mordiford on the B4224 which skirts the Woolhope Dome on its way to the south-east of the county. The ancient bridge crosses the Lugg, the second biggest river in the county, only a stone's throw from its junction with the Wye. That explains the many arches; nearly all of them are to carry away the swirling, clay-stained waters that the Lugg, when in flood, pours down its low-lying valley. The Lugg was used for carrying cargo in the past and there are still traces of docks above the bridge. Parts of the latter are more than six hundred years old, and even at that it must have had a predecessor, because in late Norman times the rent which the local lords of the manor paid to the Crown for their lands was a pair of golden spurs each time the King rode over the bridge.

The lords were the de Herefords, who (without the 'de' now) live at Sufton Court, just north of Mordiford on the road to Dormington. The late-eighteenth-century house is open to the public on Sunday afternoons in summer,

and there is an exquisite collection of antique French and Venetian lace.

Just west of Dormington the A438, the Hereford to Ledbury road, bridges first the Frome and then, at Lugwardine, the Lugg. Both rivers meet within a mile of the Wye so this is a countryside of deep water-meadows, fertile grazing and arable land. The rich farms and hamlets with intriguing names, such as Weston Beggard, Ocle Pychard, Westhide, Yarkhill, Withington and Preston Wynne, with their little churches and a few houses, stud a landscape full of rivulets.

But the key to all this fertile land east of the Lugg is the low, wooded hill which stands above the two little hamlets called Sutton St Nicholas and Sutton St Michael. It is the site of an Iron Age hill-fort known as Sutton Walls, which was occupied for more than a thousand years and was the scene of much bloodshed. Modern excavations found a number of skeletons in the ditch. Towards the end of the eighth century, Offa himself made it his headquarters while Hereford was being raised to a bishopric and extensively rebuilt. It was here, in 793, that the unfortunate King Ethelbert, to whom Hereford Cathedral is dedicated, was murdered.

The little churches at Sutton St Nicholas and Sutton St Michael have Norman fragments, but St Mary's at Marden, a mile north-east on the banks of the Lugg, must be even older. Ethelbert lay buried here until his remains were taken to Hereford, and the local legend is that water gushed from the ground where his body had lain. There is a well on the west side of the nave that is still called St Ethelbert's Well.

The Lugg is joined at Marden by the Wellington Brook, which has come trickling down the valley between the Wormsley Hills and their cornstone cousin, Dinmore. Dinmore, 'the great hill' in Welsh, towers so dramatically that the Lugg is forced into a great semicircle to maintain its southward course. The railway engineers had to drive a tunnel right through it, and the modern road twists and turns at steep gradients on either side to cross it. At the crest of this road, the A49, is a car park and cafe giving access to an arboretum which covers the hilltop plateau and is planted with trees from all parts of the world. Dinmore was bought by the Hereford branch of the Council for the Preservation of Rural England to commemorate the Silver Jubilee of King George V. The entire area is called Queen's Wood, and beside the commemorative stone are oak trees planted by Queen Elizabeth II and Prince Philip in 1957 and by her grandmother,

Queen Mary, twenty years before. All the area is open to the public, with the north and south slopes more wildly forested than the carefully attended arboretum.

From the viewpoint at the south end of the arboretum the Wellington Brook can be seen on its way to the village from which it takes its name. Wellington itself is a large working village, with half-timbered houses and farm buildings jumbled harmoniously. The church has a Norman tower and near the centre of the village is an eight-sided dovecote.

Wellington Woods cover the domed hill to the north-west, and a narrow valley that runs between these and Dinmore Woods contains the National Trust property of Dinmore Manor. This is best approached by returning to the A49 and taking a signposted lane a little further north. This was the site of the fourth largest of the fifty commanderies of the Knights Hospitallers in the country, covering parts of Shropshire, Worcestershire and Gloucestershire as well as all Herefordshire and neighbouring Welsh counties. Now there are modernized cloisters and a music room as well as splendid gardens.

The brook, in its higher reaches, passes under the road which Roman engineers swung to the west of Dinmore – the link road through the Marches known as Watling Street West (A4110). In its valley are the picturesque twin villages of Canon Pyon and King's Pyon. The unusual second name means 'gnat-infested land' and reveal how marshy this area must have been.

Ornamental dovecote at Wellington

The great bulk of Dinmore descends almost precipitously here to the Roman road from its highest point at Westhope Hill, which is well over 700 feet. Cottages built by long-ago squatters sprinkle the common land, from which there are views over a great area of north Herefordshire. There seems to be no plan in the rough, narrow lanes but an experienced map reader can find the road which runs along the scarp and then down past Bury Farm, which lies within the ramparts of an Iron Age camp. A little further on its Hope-under-Dinmore, which is separated from the A49 by its parish church. This contains a most unusual memorial to Earl and Countess Conyngsby (the same family as that responsible for the almshouse at Hereford) and their infant son who died in 1708 by choking on a cherry. The memorial, erected about fifty years later, shows the child on his mother's lap, holding the fatal cherry.

The Lugg swings sharply east nearby, to loop its way round Dinmore Hill. The main road to the south-east, the A417, follows it closely, running past Hampton Court, seen across a great well-farmed parkland. The fifteenth-century manor house, owned by such famous Herefordshire families as the Cornewalls and the Conyngsbys, was acquired in 1810 by the Arkwrights, descendants of the inventor of the spinning jenny. It is not open to the public. A mile on, at the furthest point of the Lugg's loop, is the village of Bodenham, with half-timbered and good later houses around its church and green, and the

remains of a stone cross, which stands above the river banks.

North of Dinmore, the roads that run through a land of big farms and the still bigger country estates – proud of the reputation that this is probably the best raising-ground for the white-faced, brownish-red cattle that have made the name of Herefordshire famous throughout the world – congregate at Leominster, the county's second biggest town, with a population of just over eight thousand. It was developed by Saxons on a site bounded by water to the north, east and south, and there were times when it seemed a possible challenger to Hereford as the county's religious centre but this never quite came off. Centuries later it was a challenger as a market centre to Hereford and Worcester, but these combined in adjusting market days and froze Leominster out. Now it is a thriving market town with light industry, serving the farms of this rich, well-watered area.

Leominster's name is pronounced Lemster, and is spelt like that on some of the old milestones still standing by the roads leading to the town. It is supposed to be an abbreviation of Leofric's Minster, a reference to Earl Leofric, who was the husband of Lady Godiva. Not long before the Norman Conquest, he re-established a religious house that had been set up some hundred years before.

Any remains of these buildings probably lie under the priory church, which overlooks the Lugg. The church is

141

what remains of a huge priory and the south aisle is rich with ball-flower decoration, as in several other churches in the Marches. This is a decoration used very little outside the first quarter of the fourteenth century, and consists of stone carving of a three-petalled round flower enclosing a ball. Guidebooks give architectural details but Leominster's church also contains the town's ducking stool, which was used as a punishment for 'common scolds' and for those who sold poor quality food and drink, and was last used in 1809. In the church-yard outside, careful search will reveal tombs of Sarah Siddons's grandparents, and other members of the famous acting family, the Kembles.

From the countryside around Leominster came wool which was the envy of the world for more than five hundred years. Famous authors wrote about 'Lemster ore' which came from the backs of the breed of sheep called Ryland – and there is still a Ryland Road in Leominster's suburbs.

Leominster has good Georgian buildings in Broad Street and Etnam Street but most of those before that date are in and around Corn Square. Good half-timbered work is continued down School Lane, which leads off Etnam Street opposite the town's museum, but the best work of the local woodcarvers (with one notable excep-tion) can be seen in Drapers Lane and High Street.

The exception, approached by a lane at the east end of Corn Square, is Grange Court, the finest surviving example of the craftsmanship of John Abel, the King's carpenter during the Civil War. It is a half-timbered two-storey building of intricate artistry. Now it is supported on solid masonry but originally it was on huge wooden pillars, as at Ledbury (which was also built by Abel). He built it in 1633 for the corporation's use and it stood at the top of Broad Street until it was decided that it had to go because it was an obstruction to traffic. It was sold in 1855 for just ninety-five pounds to one of the Arkwrights of Hampton Court and he had imagination enough to have it taken down and rebuilt at the Grange. It remained a private house until 1939, when there was a prospect it would be bought and exported by an American, but then Leominster Council acquired it and now use it as part of their offices.

The town's old earthworks run round the edge of the little park (which used to be Leominster Cricket Club's ground), where the war memorial bears an unexpected reference to another member of the Arkwright family. He was a local clergyman and he wrote the hymn sung at so many Armistice Day services 'O Valiant Hearts' – part of which is in bronze letters on the memorial.

The valley of the Arrow, which joins the Lugg half-a-mile south of Leominster's boundary, is the source of the route of two major roads to central Wales. They fork away from each other just west of the town, the A41 soon striking south-west and steering over the hills to the Wye Valley, Hay and Brecon, and the A44 following the line of

Corn Square at the heart of Leominster, the second largest town in Herefordshire

The main street at Dilwyn, peaceful now thanks to a bypass

the river through Kington to cross the Welsh boundary on the way to Rhayader.

The former crosses the Arrow at Monkland, so named because Benedictine monks established a cell here soon after the Conquest. The next village, Dilwyn, is bypassed but it is worth digressing to see some fine half-timbered houses, including the Great House near the church, in which is an effigy of a chain-mailed knight with his hand on his sword hilt.

A graceful fourteenth-century church spire soaring from rich meadow lands to the south of the A41 pin-points Weobley (pronounced Webley), which has such a concentration of half-timbered buildings that it is hard to think of a challenger. Five narrow roads converge on its surprisingly spacious centre. At the bottom of its sloping main street is the parish church, its size indicating the former importance of Weobley, which returned two MPs to Parliament until 1832. Monuments inside include a life-sized one on the north wall of the chancel, to Colonel John Birch, the local Civil War commander. He became an MP first for Leominster and then for Weobley – and had so many arguments with the Establishment that, he wrote later, he was imprisoned twenty-one times. He supported the return of the Monarchy, and grew in wealth and stature until his death in 1691 – but his line ended with him because both his son and daughter died before he did.

Weobley stands in the valley of the Stretford Brook,

This cruck house at Weobley is believed to be the oldest domestic building in Herefordshire

which rises a couple of miles away at Sarnesfield, at the intersection with the A41 and A480 from Stretton Sugwas. In the churchyard, just west of the main door, is the tombstone of John Abel, with a ten-line epitaph which he composed himself, full of building terms and ending with: 'his house of clay could hold no longer, May heaven's joy frame him a stronger'. And he was in his ninety-seventh year! The tombstone is too weathered to be read fully but inside the church a full version is available.

Running north-west from Sarnesfield, the A480 crosses the hills to reach the valley of the Arrow at Lyonshall, passing the village's thirteenth-century church and the castle's remains to join the A44, which crossed the river five miles out of Leominster at Eardisland. The view from the bridge here is one of the most picturesque in the Marches, with the Arrow flowing between flower-full gardens of splendidly maintained houses. The village and the lanes around it have many half-timbered houses, some dating back five or six hundred years. Best of all is the Staick House, just short of the bridge on the north side. Some parts date back to the early fourteenth century, but it is not open to the public. The Arrow flowing darkly below the bridge here is joined by a mill stream, and standing on the green peninsula of land reaching out between the two is the half-timbered Mill Stream Cottage. It was built in the seventeenth century for fifty pounds and served Eardisland for more than two hundred years as the school house. On the other side of the bridge a tall brick building with a four-gabled roof is a dovecote built about 1700. At the west end of the village a lane running south passes a thatched half-timbered house known as The Latchetts and leads on to Burton Court (open to the public on specified days in summer). It is on the site of an ancient British camp which is mentioned in Domesday Book. The entrance was redesigned in 1912 by Clough Williams-Ellis, who constructed the Italianate village of Portmeirion in North Wales, but there had been a major rebuilding in the mid nineteenth century. During this the lofty great hall, dating back to the fourteenth century, was exposed.

Eardisland's big neighbour upstream is Pembridge, which has an even greater profusion of half-timbering. There are things to admire all along its long main street – because Pembridge was granted its own market and fair in 1240. Where a side street joins the main road from a bridge across the Arrow is the old market hall, open-sided and with eight massive pillars of oak supporting a tiled roof. Behind it stone steps lead to the churchyard, the church, and a strange-looking building that has been said to resemble a pagoda. It is an eight-sided detached bell-tower, known locally as the Bell House, with thick stone walls inset with arrow-slits for defensive purposes. It has three storeys, with two tiled roofs surmounted by a thin shingled one. What is inside is even stranger. Another eight huge wooden pillars, scissor-braced, make a framework to support five bells. Experts say it is a Scandinavian style cropping up quite inexplicably in the Welsh Marches. As at Weobley, the church is surprisingly large for the size of the present township, but in the fourteenth century when most of it was built, this was a busy market town. The church's west door, now plastered over inside, bears bullet marks from Civil War fighting. The New Inn, beside the market hall, has been dated back to 1310, and the Greyhound to the early

The old schoolhouse at Eardisland, peaceful now as a private house on the banks of the Arrow

sixteenth century. Woodcarvers obviously vied with each other in the buildings, and Pembridge is also extremely rich in the more primitive cruck cottages. These were made by taking big trees with bends in them and sawing through them lengthways. Balanced against each other, each pair made wall and roof in one, meeting at the top and being well apart at the base. Cruck construction is one of the earliest forms of building using heavy timbers.

Staunton-on-Arrow, where a Roman road forded the river, is reached by minor roads off the A44 which, just beyond the Lyonshall turn, goes past Penrhos Court. There a cruck building, so old that it has thirteenth- and fourteenth-century additions, has been converted into a restaurant which brews its own beer. Kington, a mile away, is Herefordshire's most westerly market town – and the smallest with a population of some two thousand. Its long main street, rarely more than two-vehicle width, was a hazard for motorists until bypassed in the early 1980s, and it is not easy to find a place to park. But it is well worth a look round the many pleasant little shops housed in Victorian buildings which went up enthusiastically after the railway reached the town. However, the tourist has little in the way of older buildings to see except the parish church on the slopes to the west of the town, notable for one particular tomb. Its alabaster effigies represent Thomas Vaughan and his wife Ellen, known as Black Vaughan and Ellen the Terrible. He was called Black Vaughan because of the colour of his hair (his auburn-haired brother, Roger, was Red Vaughan), and Ellen earned her name because of the way she avenged her brother's death. He had been murdered so, disguised as a man, she shot an arrow through the heart of her brother's killer at an archery tournament. Thomas, born in 1400, commanded a Yorkist force defeated at the Battle of Banbury in 1469, and was captured and beheaded immediately afterwards. That was the fate of many of the leaders during the Wars of the Roses who were executed for the treason of not being on the winners' side. He and his wife lived at Hergest Court, now a farmhouse, on the lower slopes of the Hergest ridge of hills, rising some 1,400 feet to the west of Kington. His ghost, which was supposed to have returned to the Marches, was said to have been exorcized into a snuff box, and cast into the pool at Hergest Court. But it was accidentally released a century later and is still supposed to haunt the Marches in the form of a great black dog. This is claimed to be the source for *The Hound of the Baskervilles* mentioned in the last chapter – Conan Doyle is also supposed to have stayed, during his researches for this Sherlock Holmes adventure, at nearby Hergest Croft (signposted on the main road), which opens its gardens to the public in the summer months. Duke Street, in the centre of town, has some of the few half-timbered buildings remaining in Kington, including the Oxford Arms,

Buildings spanning the centuries line the road to Central Wales as it drifts through Pembridge

which has remains inside of a seventeenth-century building.

For the walker, Kington is one of the best places to pick up a magnificent section of Offa's Dyke. From Corn Square, a path across a brook leads up Bradnor Hill to the golf course, which claims to be the highest in England (so does Church Stretton in Shropshire). A marked footpath near the clubhouse leads eventually to the slopes of Rushock Hill, where the dyke can be seen crossing at nearly 1,300 feet.

The road north follows roughly the same line as the Dyke by continuing from the end of Duke Street on towards Presteigne, passing through Titley, where a Hungarian leader was buried last century. He was General Lazar Meszaros, commander-in-chief of the national army defeated by the Austrians and Russians in 1848–9. He was forced to flee into exile and chose this distant part of Herefordshire to live out the rest of his life.

Centuries of border warfare show in the way in which the national boundary departs from the line of the dyke. The English gained ground at Kington, but so did the Welsh at Presteigne. A Victorian engraved stone slab, saying 'Offa's Dyke A.D. 757', marks its crossing of the narrow road from Presteigne to Pilleth, where Owen Glendower in 1402 won the battle with an English army commanded by one of the Mortimers which brought death and destruction to the Marches. Presteigne is some three miles east of this, with the River Lugg dividing the town and marking the boundary between Wales and England. For centuries it was the assizes town for Radnorshire (incorporated since 1974 in Powys) but it remains in the diocese of Hereford, and five of the six parishes administered from the parish church are in England. In the church tower is a peal of eight bells and an eighteenth-century wooden-framed carillon claimed to be the only one of its kind still working in the country. It plays a tune at 9 a.m. and 3 p.m. each day, and curfew is still rung. Presteigne was still busy when the London-Aberystwyth stage coaches ran through it, but its importance waned when the route was changed to go through Kington, and now it has only two-thirds the population of its neighbour. A striking relic of those times is the Radnorshire Arms which was built in 1616 and became an inn in 1692. It is the black-and-white showpiece in High Street, but there are more half-timbered houses in Bridge Street, which runs off at right angles down to the Lugg. It also contains the Victorian market hall (red brick with black-and-white insets), and the nine-bayed stucco-fronted Shire Hall.

The old coach road eastward undulates over the hummocky floor of a former glacial lake, to Shobdon, a straggling village with a church that has an interior as pretty as a wedding cake. Elegant Georgian pews are painted white, picked out with china blue, and the three-decker pulpit matches. The way to it is by a road marked 'Private' opposite the Bateman Arms – named after the family that owned Shobdon Court. The Batemans are there no more, neither is their big house, but the work that the Hon. Richard Bateman had done 1752–6 – pulling down a Norman church and rebuilding it in what became known as Strawberry Hill Gothick in imitation of a new architecture in London favoured by his friend, the politician Horace Walpole – remains a delight.

The coach road plunges down to a crossroads, called Mortimer's Cross, with a milestone giving the distances to nearby local towns and to London (146 miles) and Aberystwyth (75 miles). This was an important junction in coaching days, but it was far more important on February 2, 1461 when, astride Watling Street West and hemmed in by the Lugg on the east, a battle between Yorkist and Lancastrian armies decided the monarchy of England. The Yorkists won and their leader, Edward, Earl of March, moved on to London and was crowned Edward IV. Outside a pub called The Monument on the main road a mile south is an engraved stone, erected in 1799, commemorating 'an obstinate, bloody and decisive battle'. Four thousand men are supposed to have been killed on what are now fertile fields and pieces of armour and weapons that have been found can be seen in Hereford Museum. The monument has an error in the date it gives – 1460 instead of 1461.

The monument stands on the outskirts of Kingsland, which has a lot of modern houses to accommodate people travelling to Leominster for work, but the centre of the village still has a number of excellent half-timbered buildings, notably The Angel. The church is spacious and has an unusual chapel.

A mile north of the battlefield crossroads is the little village of Aymestrey, where the Lugg turns sharply south and drives a water mill. The mill, at the east end of Mortimer's Cross bridge, is in the care of the Department of the Environment and is open to the public although approached along the drive of a private house.

Eastwards, three stately homes, all open to the public, lie within a handful of miles. The most historic is Croft Castle, standing in its mature parkland just beyond Lucton School where the white-painted wooden statue of its founder (a local boy named John Pierrepont who made good in London) stands looking out over the B4362 from a niche in the Queen Anne brickwork. There were Crofts living at Croft Castle at the time of Domesday Book and the family is still there – although there was a gap of nearly 180 years after 1746, when a Croft who was an MP had to sell the estate because of debts. Now it is National Trust property. Rooms furnished with family treasures are open to the public, a footpath leads to the Iron Age fort of Croft Ambrey, and in the grounds is a magnificent avenue of sweet-chestnut trees – said by some to have been planted in the formation of the Spanish Armada, and by others to have grown from chestnuts which came from the Spanish galleons. The service the Crofts have given their country is probably best summed up in the little church adjoining the castle, where on the south wall near the altar are two marble plaques. One is to the tenth baronet, Sir Herbert Croft; the other to the eleventh baronet, his son, Sir James Herbert Croft. Each enlisted in the Herefordshire Regiment at the outbreak of war, and was a captain when killed on active service – the tenth baronet at Gallipoli in 1915, the eleventh in 1941 while serving with No. 1 Commando. More than eight hundred years before, their forebear, Jasper de Croft, was knighted for his part in the taking of Jerusalem during the Crusades.

Opposite the entrance to Croft Castle, a lane leads to Yarpole, where the church has a detached bell-tower which is a cousin to that at Pembridge. It is smaller, of only two storeys, and has inside four great oak beams, looking as though they had grown in position and then been adzed into shape; they support two bells. On the other side of the old coach road between Leominster and Ludlow, now the B4361, at the entrance to the village of Luston, a lane leads to the other two stately homes standing almost cheek by jowl. Just east of the main Hereford-Shrewsbury railway line is the privately-owned Eye Manor (open to the public), which from the outside looks like just a big brick house, but inside it is a different matter. The house was built by a man called Ferdinando Gorges, who made a fortune in the Barbados trade in slaves and sugar, and who was known in those days as the King of the Black Market. He spared no expense on large-panelled plaster ceilings in nearly every room, exquisitely decorated.

In the little Norman church at Eye are memorials to three brothers killed in the First World War (all of them officers and two of them MPs). They were sons of the first Lord Cawley, owner since 1901 of Berrington Hall, a National Trust property a little further along the same minor road. It was built towards the end of the eighteenth century of a pinkish sandstone quarried a few hundred yards away, and after two hundred years it remains almost as it was planned and decorated. The large ground-floor rooms have superbly painted ceilings and the staircase is magnificent. 'Capability' Brown landscaped its 455 acres of parkland, including a seventeen-acre lake for which he dammed a tiny rivulet.

Iron railings fence Berrington's Park for a mile along each side of the A49, the road leading to the valley of the Teme. Just south of them is the A4112, the road from Leominster to Tenbury which crosses a minor Roman road and then runs along the crest of a sandstone ridge through farmlands served by isolated churches – Middleton-on-the-Hill, Kimbolton, Puddleston and finally Leysters. Here at Leysters Pole a steep slope takes the road into Worcestershire.

CHAPTER ELEVEN

Stronghold of the Mortimers

From the bubbling spring that has its source in the sheep-walks of the Kerry Hills in mid-Wales to the water-meadows of the Severn at Powick is something like seventy miles as the Teme flows, with long, uninterrupted stretches in Shropshire, Herefordshire and Worcestershire. It is a different matter though, at Tenbury Wells, where the county boundaries dance about the river almost like the mayflies on its surface in early summer. In a five-mile stretch the Teme runs through all three counties with a central section where Shropshire is on the north bank and Worcestershire on the south, the middle of the river being the boundary.

A curving six-arched bridge – the three northern arches are medieval – links Tenbury with Burford, the Shropshire part of the town with the fruit-processing industry, and the hospital and the former railway station. Tenbury, Worcestershire's smallest market town, was also formerly its smallest spa, hence the 'Wells' in the name. A spring of saline water was discovered in 1830 and a pump room and bath house were built in 1862 and extended in 1911. Somewhat deprecatingly, the owners advertised it as a spa for 'middling and working classes' offering 'every convenience at the lowest possible price'. The spa never recovered after the First World War and the rusting structure of its buildings, locally known as the Pepper Pot, stands forlornly near the Crow Hotel on the banks of the Kyre Brook at the south end of Teme Street.

Tenbury's parish church was rebuilt in 1770 after one of its pillars had been undermined by the Teme in flood and collapsed, and apart from a few timber-framed buildings there is little of architectural interest in the sleepy streets. A folksy, oval market house built in 1811 stands in the triangular market place. Tenbury is at its most bustling on the four or five Tuesdays before Christmas, when the streets are full of lorries laden with local-grown holly and mistletoe, sold by auction to buyers from many parts of the country.

South-west of Tenbury is St Michael's, a prep school specializing in music which has a library of more than

The rusting remains of the spa at Tenbury Wells

eight thousand scores, including the original one that Handel used while conducting the first performance of the *Messiah*. Not far away are Bockleton, where a memorial in the church commemorates a 25-year-old man who died after visiting his aged gamekeeper who was mortally ill with fever, and Kyre Magna, which claims to have had the oldest Anglican vicar on record – the Rev. Hugo Thomas, who had been its vicar for sixty years when he died in 1693 aged 107.

The main road between the Midlands and West and Central Wales, the A456, runs past the north end of Tenbury Bridge using a valley the narrowness of which becomes apparent at Newnham Bridge. The trunk road crosses the River Rea – just about to join the Teme after running through Cleobury Mortimer and Neen Sollars – and is then joined at a Georgian coaching house by the Worcester road, the A443. The embankment of the old Wyre Forest Railway looms above, and behind it are traces of the canal that carried coal from the Mamble pits to Leominster. On the Rea here is a water-mill that still grinds corn and is open at weekends in summer.

The steep slopes northwards are the foothills of Titterstone Clee, the peak of which is 1,749 feet. There are steep gradients in the narrow roads and lanes that edge their way from rich farmlands and a handful of hamlets to gorsy common land where sheep and ponies range free. The main road between Bewdley and Ludlow, the A4117, crosses the Clee at heights of up to 1,300 feet, giving panoramic views over the Teme Valley as far as the Malverns and the Black Mountains. One clutch of little settlements consists of Knighton-on-Teme (rather a misnomer, since the Teme is at least two miles away), Milson and Coreley. Boraston has an unusually high wooden spire. Straddling the main Tenbury road to Titterstone are Greete, Nash and Whitton, with the latter having a stained-glass window by William Morris and Sir Edward Burne-Jones, associates in the Victorian Pre-Raphaelite Brotherhood. All three have Norman remains in their Victorian-restored churches, as has Hope Bagot, where the lanes are worn deep by the feet of countless pilgrims visiting a spring, near the church, that was reputed to cure blindness.

Knowbury and Doddington, higher up the slopes, developed in the middle of the last century as mining communities and became more extensive as squatters enclosed more and more pieces of land. Highest of all is Clee Hill village, exposed to all weathers and claiming that no settlement southwards is at such an altitude – approximately 1,150 feet above sea level. It developed to serve the dhu-stone quarries on the higher slopes. The stone (dhu is from the Welsh word meaning 'black') is a hard-wearing volcanic rock much used for road metal, and caps of it prevented Titterstone and Brown Clee from being worn away by erosion. It is claimed that seventeen counties can be seen from the top of Titterstone, where

Shingled church spire at Boraston

there is a huge Iron Age fort covering more than seventy acres.

On the lower western slopes is Bitterley, in 1712 important enough for a former headmaster of Eton College to found a grammar school there that lasted for more than two hundred years. In the churchyard is a remarkably well-preserved fourteenth-century cross with most of its stone lantern (always the first target for the Puritans), and the church has solid Elizabethan and Jacobean furnishings. Caynham, on the south-west slopes, retains a striking chancel arch as well as other Norman remains, and overlooking it is an Iron Age fort, still with earth walls up to twenty feet high, called Caynham Camp. Below it, the Ledwyche Brook cascades over a weir on its way to join the Teme at Burford, where it marks the county boundary between Shropshire and Herefordshire. This is in the old part of Burford, where the church contains a monument to a princess (one of John of Gaunt's daughters) and a most remarkable memorial to one of the Cornewalls, lords of the manor for centuries. He was Richard, who died in 1563, and he, his mother and his father are remembered in three painted panels joined together and eleven feet tall.

The main road west passes between Shropshire's only two hopfields and then a little Norman church in the fields at Little Hereford, so named because it once belonged to monks at Hereford Cathedral. Then the A456 kinks across the Teme over a five-arched bridge

The preaching cross at Bitterley that escaped the attentions of both the Reformation and Puritanism

built in 1761 and soon divides into a road to Woofferton – once the terminus of the old Wyre Forest Railway and now a BBC transmitting station – and another to Brimfield, where the village church stands on a ridge that greatly affected the landscape. It runs two miles westwards to Orleton, and it consists of the moraine left by a glacier some 25,000 years ago. It blocked the course that the Teme took southwards to the Wye and diverted it eastwards to the Severn.

Tucked-away Orleton has a flood of modern houses, but also a picturesque street winding from the half-timbered manor house to the church, which has another of the fonts carved by the Herefordshire School. It consists of nine men under arches, believed to represent Apostles.

Westwards, running below hills more than one thousand feet high, is the B4361, the old main road between Leominster and Ludlow that was called The Portway. Boundary vagaries occur again at Richard's Castle, where the village pub and the old church are in Herefordshire, the village hall and the new church in Shropshire. All Saints, beside the road, was completed in 1892; St Bartholomew's, high in the hills above, is Norman with medieval and Tudor additions. Because Victorian attention was focused on All Saints, the latter escaped restoration and looks much as it did in Georgian times, with box pews. A square, detached bell-tower stands beside it, obviously intended for defence if need

be. The wood above it contains one of the two remaining sites in Herefordshire of a pre-Conquest Norman castle (the other is at Ewyas Harold in the Black Mountains). It was built soon after 1050 by Richard le Scrob, and some of his stone walls and the gateway, and the sixty-foot-high motte can still be seen, even though obscured by undergrowth. A planned town grew up under the castle's protection, and lasted for more than three hundred years. Even now, much of the town's walls can be traced, and a little triangle of grass remains of what was the market place.

In the valley below, the Teme lazes between Ashford Carbonell, where the Norman church has an unusual oval window pointed at each end, and tiny Ashford Bowdler, recovering from its buffeting over the weirs and rapids at Ludlow. Here the river is forced to turn nearly half-a-circle by hard Silurian rocks, through a gorge with heavily wooded, almost precipitous slopes on the one side and the town enclosed inside the loop on the other, well back from risks of flood.

At the top of the wooded hill, Whitcliffe (Ludlow's common land by gift since 1221) provides the classic overall view of the castle, church tower and town, with Titterstone and Brown Clee in the background and the Stretton Hills to the north. The Norman castle, overlooking the Teme and its tributary river the Corve from a steep-sided spur of hard rock, was built in the years around 1090. Under its protection, a planned town soon sprouted, with main streets running down the south-facing slopes to the fast-flowing Teme, the waters of which drove the mills that made Ludlow into a medieval manufacturing town, specializing in woollen cloth. The castle was greatly enlarged in the middle of the four-teenth century by one of the Mortimers, distant relations of William I, who had gained Ludlow by marriage, and who became the Earls of March. They were leaders of the Yorkists during the Wars of the Roses and although Ludlow was sacked by the opposing Lancastrians in 1459, it received its reward two years later from Edward IV after his victory at Mortimer's Cross. He gave the town from which he had marched out to battle a liberal charter, including an annual fair on May 1 – and Ludlow May Fair still takes place on that date in the streets outside the castle gates.

Even greater benefits followed his decision to make Ludlow Castle the seat of the Court and Council of the Marches of Wales, governing five English counties as well as all Wales. This brought prosperity and prestige to the town which still remembers in its coat-of-arms, three white roses of York around the silver lion of March. The Council lasted for more than two hundred years, until 1689, and big houses that remain tell of the wealth of its officials. Even larger houses were built during Georgian times, when Ludlow became the fashionable centre for the local aristocracy and gentry. But with railways making travel easier – and a recession in its local industries – Ludlow practically fossilized in the mid nine-teenth century. There has been little building since within the mile-long circuit of the town walls, of which about three-quarters remain – a point made by Alec Clifton-Taylor when he ended his BBC television series on English country towns with Ludlow.

Since 1980, Ludlow has been bypassed to the east by the A49, taking the weight of trunk-road traffic away from the fourteenth-century Ludford Bridge, under which the Teme surges at the gorge's narrowest point. On the south bank is the charming little backwater of Ludford, with the coloured tomb of Sir Job Charlton – Speaker of the House of Commons, who died in 1697 – in its Norman church.

On the north side Ludlow's idiosyncrasies begin to show in a street which runs up to the town walls that existed before these were built in the thirteenth century. This is Lower Broad Street, with houses on the west side which are well below road-level. At the top is the Broad Gate – the only one of Ludlow's seven gates to have survived – which is so low and narrow that a single-decker bus can only just scrape through. It still has its portcullis-slot and medieval drum-towers, but on top is a spacious brick house built in the eighteenth century. At the side is a medieval public house backing on to the town wall.

Through the gate is Upper Broad Street, widely praised in superlatives as perhaps the finest street in the

Ludlow climbing uphill beyond medieval Ludford Bridge to the narrow Broad Gate

country. Along stone pavements raised above cobbled slopes stand gracious houses with fronts of brick, stucco or stone, culminating in a wealth of black-and-white at the Butter Cross. This is the heart of Ludlow as a living town that has survived change – a masterly hotchpotch of buildings that went up through many centuries with no master-plan, but all living happily together.

The Norman planners originally made a wide market place along the crest of the ridge, from the castle to what is now called the Bull Ring, where it met a minor Roman road superimposed on a prehistoric track (the present Old Street and Corve Street). Now, going eastwards from the castle, first comes the much-criticized town hall, built in 1887 to commemorate the Golden Jubilee of Queen Victoria, on the site of a brick predecessor. Then come four streets jammed in lengthways, the sites of medieval shops that replaced temporary stalls in the market place. High Street is wide enough for two vehicles for most of its length, Church Street and Market Street for one each, and Harp Lane is a pedestrian throughway. Then come more encroachments, which mean that a large vehicle can only just squeeze between the eighteenth-century Butter Cross and the fifteenth-century overhanging, half-timbered corner shop. Then it shrinks into The Narrows, with less than nine feet between the pavements, before reaching the Bull Ring.

Recent research of many old documents has produced some excellent guide books, notably that for St Laurence's, one of the six largest parish churches in the country. Its tower, 132 feet high and reached by climbing 202 steps, dominates the surrounding countryside – and the church is more than 200 feet long. Its treasures include misericords which range from references to a crowned king to the treatment of a dishonest alewife, flamboyant tombs of notables connected with the Council of the Marches, and the huge, glowing windows, many of them containing medieval glass. The central west window, of Victorian glass, shows major figures connected with Ludlow Castle: Edward IV, his son Edward V (the elder of the two little princes murdered in the Tower) and Prince Arthur, Henry VIII's elder brother, who died in the castle, probably of pneumonia when 16, soon after his marriage to Catherine of Aragon.

Outside the church, at the west end of the north wall, is a tablet commemorating A.E. Housman, whose ashes lie below the bells which play a different tune each day of the week, still adhering to what he noted in:

Or come you home of Monday
When Ludlow market hums
And Ludlow chimes are playing
"The conquering hero comes",

The tablet in the wall beside his is to Ludlow-born Adrian Jones, sculptor of the four giant rearing horses known as The Quadriga on Constitution Hill, London.

Another of his huge chargers is in the upper storey of Ludlow Town Hall.

An excellent town trail prepared by Shropshire County Museum Department – Ludlow's own museum is in the upper storey of the Butter Cross – says the route it details through the streets, lanes, and medieval passageways can be done in 1½ hours, but it recommends a day, with three-quarters of an hour for the church and an hour for the castle. Main features of this are the original keep, the round nave of a Norman chapel (there are only four others in the country), and the shell of the great hall, in which Milton's masque, *Comus*, which he wrote while a tutor at the castle, was first performed. All are reached from the inner bailey, where Ludlow Festival's annual Shakespeare production takes place. The walk circling the castle emphasizes the steepness of the site, the way in which the walls tower skywards from the bedrock of which they are built and the water defences.

That bedrock has done more for Ludlow than provide vast quantities of the building stone everywhere evident in the old town; it has put it on the world's geological map. The hills west of the Teme – the castle is on an outcrop – are of the same limestone, and it is common along most of the Marches. Quarries and woodland roads teeming with fossils that were deposited on a sea-bed four hundred million years ago have been opened for walkers. These are signposted by the Forestry Commission in Mortimer Forest (just beyond Whitcliffe), and in 1981 this was named as the international section of the world-wide Ludlow Series of the Silurian System. Geologists come from far and wide to inspect it, and fossils from it are in Ludlow Museum.

Millions of conifers – planted after the Second World War and ousting oaks through being a quicker cash crop – manage to flourish on the thin soil. But it is a different matter east of the Teme, where they mark a sharp division between limestone and the softer sandstone. Here, instead of the soil being yellowish-grey, it is the red of much of Herefordshire, which in turn smacks of Devon because basically all derive from the Old Red Sandstone, although geologists still argue about precise demarcation lines.

The result in this part of the Shropshire/Herefordshire border is a land of very mixed farming, typical of so much of the Middle Marches: sheep and fir trees on the high land; cattle, potatoes, soft fruit, corn and hay in the valleys; fallow deer in the forest; and game-fish in the rivers and streams – so unpolluted that even the fastidious grayling flourishes. And all this within three or four miles of town.

One of the rivers is the Corve, which joins the Teme below Ludlow Castle. On its banks, three miles upstream, is Stanton Lacy, at the heart of the huge Saxon manor where the idea of a Norman castle at Ludlow germinated. After the Conquest it was granted to Walter

Building style contrasts in Ludlow; seventeenth-century half-timbering on a medieval stone base; Norman castle keep; Victorian town hall

de Lacy (the man who fell to his death from St Peter's, Hereford) and his son Roger chose the site of Ludlow Castle. Stanton Lacy Church has Saxon work, easily seen in the long, flat slabs in the north and west outside walls.

Two prehistoric burial barrows show the age of the nearby Old Field (now used as Ludlow racecourse and golf course), on the other side of which is Bromfield, where the Teme is joined by the River Onny. This is near the parish church which has a remarkable seventeenth-century folk-art painted ceiling in the chancel – all angels and clouds and texts. St Mary's is what remains of a Benedictine priory's church which was converted into a private house after the Dissolution and remained so until 1658. Just beyond the lych gate is the gatehouse of the old priory, ancient timbers capping its thick stone walls.

At Bromfield the A4113 leaves the A49 to connect with the Teme Valley again at Leintwardine. Until the middle of the eighteenth century it followed the river's course more closely, but then was diverted to avoid detracting from Downton Castle, which was being built by Richard Payne Knight, who collaborated with Sir Uvedale Price (see Chapter 9) in 'naturalistic' building and landscaping. His grandfather had made a fortune in iron in the Severn Gorge and had bought large estates in this part of Herefordshire, and Payne Knight, for his mansion-cum-castle, chose a site overlooking the Teme rushing through a limestone gorge under the towering heights of Bringewood Chase. Downton Castle is not open to the public but an idea of the scenery can be gained at Bow Bridge, near Downton-on-the-Rock.

Here the Teme carved a way out after a glacier's debris had blocked its course at Aymestrey, impounding its waters in what is now the Vale of Wigmore. Farms that developed on the soil of the old lake-bed were served by a handful of Norman churches. That at Burrington has well-preserved iron gravestones, dating between 1619 and 1754 (probably cast at a local foundry of the Knights), on the ground outside its east window. That at Pipe Aston is still practically all Norman, with a Lamb of God on its tympanum. Elton's has a coat of arms of Elizabeth I carved in wood, and at adjoining Elton Hall Richard Payne Knight's brother, Thomas Andrew Knight, spent more than twenty-five years developing fruit-trees, notably cherries (and the Black Elton is still grown in Worcestershire cherry orchards). He was also a geologist, and a fossil shell long known as *Conchidium Knightii*, makes up most of the limestone quarried at nearby Leinthall Earls – twin village to Leinthall Starkes, which straggles so far along the road east of Wigmore that it is locally known as 'Long Leinthall'.

Wigmore, capital of the hill-ringed vale, is now a peaceful village with a wide main street that was the market place, but it knew stirring times when it was the stronghold of the Mortimers before they moved to Ludlow. The remains of their castle are half-a-mile along Church Lane, which runs from the main street past St

James's, a church with early Norman remains perched on a knoll so steep that it is a defensive position in itself.

West of the A4110, the tumbled hills of sparsely populated Deerfold Forest climb to more than twelve hundred feet at the Welsh border. Two miles north of Wigmore, a lane marked to Burrington and Downton turns off right to Grange Farm, which incorporates remnants of Wigmore Abbey. Inside the imposing gate-house, similar to that at Bromfield only larger, is a tablet which says: 'In this abbey lie the remains of the noble family of Mortimer who founded it in 1179 and ruled the Marches of Wales for 400 years.' It names the thirteen in the male succession, which ended when the last one died a bachelor, and ends '. . . and finally destroyed by King Henry VIII in 1538'. Henry's mother was a Mortimer, a daughter of Edward IV, but he showed no respect for her ancestors' tombs – they have all vanished.

The lane on from Grange Farm follows the track of the Roman road, Watling Street West, to Leintwardine, where the Teme is joined by another of its larger tribu-taries, the River Clun. Building on either side of the main road that runs through the village has almost obliterated traces of the Roman town of Bravonium, but the parish church provides a clue. The chancel is unusually higher than the nave, because it is built on what was the eastern rampart of the old town.

On the road to Knighton is the last Herefordshire village on the Teme, Brampton Bryan. The hall, home of the Harleys (whose interests in London resulted in Harley Street and Wigmore Street – and hence the Wigmore Hall) stands on the site of a castle destroyed during the Civil War in spite of a valiant defence led by Lady Brilliana Harley, whose husband was away serving Parliament. The adjoining church was also destroyed during the siege, and had to be rebuilt, which is why it looks so bare and Puritan.

The rounded hill to the north, rising steeply on the far bank of the Teme, is Coxall Knoll, widely regarded as the scene of the last stand of the British chief Caractacus against the Romans. The hill also overshadows Bucknell, through which the little River Redlake babbles and where the church has a font so old that it could be Saxon.

Herefordshire ends just to the west and the Teme becomes the boundary between Shropshire and Wales, crossing Offa's Dyke at Knighton, which is astride the dyke and has the Welsh name of Tref-y-Clawdd ('The Town on the Dyke'). Although its population is only about two thousand, Knighton is the second largest town in Radnorshire (now in Powys) – with the reservation that some of the town, including the railway station, is in Shropshire. Its main street is as steep as that of many a seaside fishing village, with a Victorian clock-tower and a small triangular market place halfway up. The George and Dragon Hotel, dating back to 1637, is just below the clock-tower, as is The Little House, a narrow timber-framed house built in the fifteenth century. Otherwise,

The Lion Hotel at Leintwardine (the Roman town of Bravonium) seen across the village green

Knighton's central buildings are late-Victorian onwards, including a school which is now a Welsh Border information centre and youth hostel. From it a path runs down to a footbridge, at the railway station, that crosses the Teme and climbs steep Panpunton Hill. Then it picks up the line of the Offa's Dyke Path – striding over the high land to Clun, with views to the west of the Teme winding out of Wales at Llanfairwaterdine, and going under the first bridge that dares to challenge its tumbling waters.

CHAPTER TWELVE

Over the Hills and Back Again

Twisting and turning up hill and down dale, the A488 runs northwards towards Clun with a huge 'ER' clearly visible on the wood-covered slopes to the left. When the wood was planted in the early 1950s, a different type of conifer was used to pick out the initials of 'Elizabeth Regina' to mark the Queen's accession.

Although often running at well over eight hundred feet above sea level, the road is frequently overtopped by hills which have traces of Man going right back to the Stone Age. At the signposted Five Turnings, a lane leads to a hill called Caer Caradoc (meaning 'the fort of Caractacus'), not far from Coxall Knoll, and flint tools and weapons turn up by the thousand round about.

This is because Stone Age trading tracks converged in the Clun Valley, now peaceful but for centuries the setting for fierce fighting. In coaching days, too, it was busy as part of the route leading through central Wales to Aberystwyth and Holyhead. This is now the B4368, which leads past an isolated inn called The Anchor, so far

west of Offa's Dyke that Cardigan Bay is only thirty-five miles away as the crow flies.

There are six place-names in the valley that include a river's name. The nearest to Wales is Newcastle-on-Clun, with a handful of houses, a Victorian church and a pleasant pub but no trace remaining of the 'new castle' after which the hamlet was named. Half-a-mile east the road cuts spectacularly through the dyke at Lower Spoad Farm (named after a family owning it, one male member of which went to Staffordshire, altered the spelling to 'Spode', and made a fortune in bone china). The farmhouse is exceedingly old and one of the fireplaces has a massive wooden overmantel. On this is a carving of a man about to shoot an arrow into a deer jumping over the pit in which he is lying. This was a method of hunting made punishable by death by the Normans, so the age of the carving is anyone's guess. The earth bank of the dyke, toweringly high in the farmyard, continues on the other side of the road to cross the river valley and stride on northwards along the bare hillsides.

Clun township itself is a couple of miles east of the dyke, clustered on riverside slopes which are linked by a narrow, five-arched medieval bridge which has tiny cut-waters. It grew up to serve a castle built about 1100 by a Norman, Picot de Say – although the site was so exposed that the infant town was burnt down at least four times by the Welsh and once by King John in punitive warfare against rebellious barons. The castle later passed by marriage to ancestors of the present dukes of Norfolk, who still include 'Baron of Clun' in their title. Most of the massive keep stands on the strategically important hill overlooking the junction of the tiny River Unk with the Clun, but much of the castle's locally quarried stone has gone into the older local domestic buildings.

One of the best of these is the eighteenth-century town hall in the square, with details outside of how to obtain admission to see its outstanding collection of flint and stone implements found locally. Sir Walter Scott stayed at the fishing inn on the other side of the square while researching for his historical novel *The Betrothed*, published in 1825, for which Clun Castle is believed to be the model for Garde Doloreux.

Clun Church's Norman tower, which looks down on the bridge from the other side of the river, was so strongly built that it withstood any attempts to raze it. Perhaps the rest of the church did too – but during the Civil War, the Royalists attacking Parliamentary troops inside caused such damage that Charles II, after the Restoration, performed the rare act of ordering a special collection for repairs.

Feelings ran high in the Clun Valley during the struggle between King and Parliament. Depredations by the soldiers on both sides were so great that local people banded together and armed themselves, even before the farmers in Worcestershire, and became known as the Clubmen of Clun. They grew strong enough to control the warring troops – but not before one of the most barbarous acts of the Civil War had taken place at nearby Hopton Castle.

This lies under the towering slopes of Hopton Titterill, between the Clun and the Teme. It was garrisoned by forty Roundheads, who beat off attacks by vastly superior forces until cannon were brought up and they surrendered. Under a then rule-of-war which was supposed to reduce casualties – that those defending an untenable position could expect no mercy – all except the commander were executed on the spot. The Royalists said they were shot; the Roundheads that they were tied back to back, mutilated so that they could not swim and then thrown into the moat to drown. The commander whose orders they had obeyed was taken as a prisoner to Ludlow Castle.

The remains of Hopton Castle (which are on private ground but can be seen from the roadside) now stand in as peaceful a setting as any in the valley, like the neighbouring hamlets mentioned in the local jingle 'Clunton

Clun Castle, which Sir Walter Scott used as his model for Garde Doloreux

and Clunbury, Clungunford and Clun, Are the quietest places Under the sun', which caused Housman to write one of his saddest poems, starting:

In valleys of springs of rivers,
By Onny and Teme and Clun,
The country for easy livers,
The quietest under the sun.

Clungunford is the largest of them, and probably the oldest, with a Bronze Age tumulus near the church. It has been excavated and finds are on view in Clun Museum.

Astride the B4368 as it heads eastwards for the A49, while the Clun dips southwards to Leintwardine, is Aston-on-Clun, which has a public house called The Kangaroo (an incongruous name for this part of the country). An old half-dead tree on the north side of the road commemorates a wedding that took place on May 29, 1786. The villagers hung flags on it for their squire's wedding, and his family supplied fresh ones for it each year until they died out in 1951. Since then the flags, which are left on the tree all the year round and are torn to tatters by the winter gales, have been supplied by the parish of Hopesay, of which Aston-on-Clun is a part.

Hopesay lies on the lower slopes of the medley of hills that separates the Clun and Onny valleys, and has a church tower that is a smaller version of the massive one at Clun (the second syllable of the place name recalls the de Says, whose territory spread down the Clun Valley

and beyond). Nearer the Onny Valley is Lydbury North, where the church is notable for two large chapels, the Plowden and the Walcot, for the two large local estates. The Plowdens, who adhered to the old faith throughout the Reformation and later persecutions, have lived for centuries at Plowden Hall, which has several priests' holes. The Walcot estate was bought by Robert Clive with some of the fortune he brought back from India towards the end of the eighteenth century – and he had the name of one of his famous battles, Plassey, spelt out in trees in the grounds.

Long before the Conquest, a Saxon lord gave the huge parish of Lydbury North (some seventeen hundred acres) to the bishops of Hereford in gratitude at being miraculously cured of the palsy, but Norman churchmen decided there was a strategically stronger site three miles west. They built what by the thirteenth century was known as the Bishop's Castle – still the name of what was the smallest borough in England (population twelve hundred) until it lost that status in local government reorganization in 1967. To show the sparseness of the population in this south-west corner of Shropshire, even when it was joined with the rural district of Clun, there were still only just over ten thousand people in an area of more than 130,000 acres.

Basically, Bishop's Castle is a long High Street, plus a Norman grid-iron pattern of smaller streets now containing mostly Georgian and Victorian houses. The church, much restored but with an interesting memorial to a French cavalry officer who died while a prisoner-of-war during the Napoleonic Wars, is at the bottom of the hill. The castle was at the top, but all that remains is a fragment of wall in the car park of the hotel that now stands on the site. Just below is the town's most impressive building, the eighteenth-century stone-built town hall, with two iron-barred round windows on the ground floor that seem like eyes gazing straight down the slope to the church. They are, in fact, the windows of what was the local lock-up. A path at the side of the town hall, paved with notably small cobbles, leads under the best of Bishop's Castle's half-timbered buildings, the House on Crutches – an apt name because part of the first storey straddles the path on two stout wooden pillars. On the other side of the town hall, Salop Street contains the Three Tuns, which won national fame in the mid-1970s when campaigners for real ale discovered that it was still producing home-brew.

On the other side of the street is a puzzlingly large open space – shrubbed, paved and be-stepped, and dominated by a large stone slab carved with a coat-of-arms supported by elephants. The old market hall stood here, and when it was demolished the stone depicting the arms of the Clives that had been on the first-floor exterior was taken and used as an eye-catcher. Hence the elephant – because the famous Robert Clive made nearby Walcot Hall the family seat when he returned rich and triumphant from India in the 1760s.

Bishop's Castle was once the terminus of perhaps the least successful railway in the country after the most unpropitious of openings. When the first train arrived, the passengers found the station had not been completed – and it was two months before the next train ran. In its seventy years (it closed in 1935) it never made an annual profit. Yet its nine-mile track to the main line at Craven Arms was a brilliant feat of engineering, with the route having to follow the writhings of the Onny through the Plowden Gorge before finding more open country north of the terminus, at Lydham.

This is just a handful of buildings where the A488 and the A489 coalesce for a short distance before the former strikes north for Shrewsbury and the latter heads on for central Wales and Cardigan Bay. But Lydham has its history. The Saxon owner of the manor fought on against the Normans after the Conquest, and although eventually dispossessed, he supposedly haunts the district. Locals say that Wild Edric and the fairy he married still hunt the land around with a pack of phantom hounds.

Perhaps the eeriness of the landscape northwards contributes to this. It is the Shropshire lead country, mined from Roman times – there is a pig of the metal, bearing the stamp of the Emperor Hadrian, in Shrewsbury Museum – until the end of the last century, when discoveries in other continents made the mines uneconomic.

The tumbledown buildings and the spoil-heaps of abandoned mines scar the landscape, but towering over it all is the stark shape of the Stiperstones. Jagged crags silhouetted against the skyline make this ridge look like the armoured back of some giant reptile from prehistory, although the rocks of the Stiperstones are immeasurably older – something like 500 million years. They are whitish in colour, formed of the compressed sand of an ancient seashore. The Ice Age shattered the rock into blocks of which the smaller rolled down the hill, making walking almost impossible except along the worn sheep-tracks, but providing a refuge among the heather and whinberry cover for wildlife, including grouse. The great crags on the crest, which at its highest point reaches 1,731 feet (making it the third highest point in the county, after the two Clees) have individual names, such as Cranberry Rock and Nipstone Rock. The one just west of the Ordnance Survey marker is the Devil's Chair, where Old Nick is supposed to sit during thunderstorms, glorying in the noise and flashes of lightning.

Mary Webb, who became a cult figure in the 1930s, set her novels hereabout. In *The Golden Arrow*, Diafol Mountain ('diafol' is Welsh for 'devil') is clearly the Stiperstones. And in *Gone to Earth* – a 1948 film made on location in Shropshire, starring Jennifer Jones and David Farrar – the heroine, Hazel Woodus, plunged to her death with her pet fox in her arms down a mine shaft just like the one by the crossroads at Pennerley.

This stands at one end of the wild unfenced road that crosses the Stiperstones just below the crags (the other end is at Ratlinghope). It is a key point to the maze of lanes that wriggle through hills in which men from the Stone, Bronze and Iron Ages have left traces. The Romans built here, too; a piece of mosaic work from one of their villas excavated in the 1960s is in the floor near the font of More Church. The villa was in the grounds of Linley Hall on the slopes of Linley Hill, where one of the More family planted the first larch trees to be brought to Britain, in 1738. The Mores, who came over with the Conqueror, have provided national figures down the centuries, the most recent Sir Jasper, a long-serving Member of Parliament until 1979.

More village, which has pleasant half-timbered houses, is on the little river called the West Onny which unites with the East Onny to form the Onny proper at the entrance to the Plowden Gorge. Near here a narrow road that gives access to the minute hamlets of Norbury, Myndtown and Wentnor follows the East Onny's valley through the gap between the Stiperstones and the Longmynd, a great plateau (mostly National Trust) of rocks more than a thousand million years old. The name is a hybrid, the second syllable being an abbreviation of 'mynydd', the Welsh for 'mountain'. Along the road is Ratlinghope, pronounced 'ratchup', an ancient settlement at the very heart of these Shropshire highlands, with the convenience of an inn and a youth hostel.

A narrow road, unfenced for much of the way and with nearly precipitous drops at times, leads from Ratlinghope to Church Stretton over the Longmynd, crossing the prehistoric track called The Portway, which runs the length of the plateau. The poor, thin soil supports little but whinberry bushes, heather, gorse and heathland grasses, with practically no cover – and although it is a wonderful place to explore in good weather, it can be fiercely treacherous, especially in winter.

For instance, in Woolstaston Church at the Longmynd's northern edge is a memorial to a clergyman who used to walk to Ratlinghope and back on Sunday afternoons to take a service. On January 29, 1865, he was overtaken by a blizzard soon after starting his return journey. He knew he had to keep walking to stay alive and twenty-two hours later – exhausted, injured by falls, snow-blind and frost-bitten – he stumbled into some cottages at Church Stretton, right off his route. His worn-out shoes are on display in Shrewsbury Museum.

The Longmynd's scarp is so steep above the Onny Valley that there is only one other access point for vehicles – at Asterton, where a one-in-four gradient road leads to the airfield for gliders it was built to serve. Downriver the old railway crossed to the south bank to squeeze through to Craven Arms, the only town in the county to come into existence because of railways – after

Ludlow had refused to become a junction. When the Hereford/Shrewsbury track was routed this way in the 1850s, a junction was established to serve lines through central Wales and to the Severn Gorge (along the foot of Wenlock Edge) and Bishop's Castle. The local landowner, the Earl of Craven, saw the chance of establishing a market town and 'planted' a grid-iron of shops and houses, on Norman lines. The result has been described as 'like a prairie town and just as ugly', but its sheep sales, particularly those in autumn, are famous along the Marches. The town has the peculiar distinction of being named after the railway station, which in its turn took its title from the only building near it when it was constructed, a coaching inn called The Craven Arms. This stands where the road from Clun joins the A49, with a reminder on the opposite corner of the old coaching days – a twenty-foot obelisk giving the distances to no fewer than thirty-six cities and towns, including London, Edinburgh and Plymouth. It dates back to the turn of the eighteenth century when turnpike laws made markers stating mileages essential. The obelisk is probably the second oldest piece of building in Craven Arms. The oldest must be the little church of Halford parish, overrun by the new town's development to the north-east, where the Norman entrance arch is carved with what Pevsner describes as 'crocus blossoms' (probably the autumn crocus, cultivated since Roman times for the saffron its stamen provides).

Most of Craven Arms is in the parish of Stokesay (another de Saye ending, as at Hopesay). Half-a-mile south of the town on the A49 is a picture-book setting of medieval manor house, church and farm, with a great wooded hill on each side and the Onny flowing past to find a way to the Teme at Onibury – where in the church are two seventeenth-century cast-iron tomb slabs, left and right of the altar. Stokesay Castle (open to the public most of the year) is one of the finest fortified manor houses in the country, built about 1275 with windows so huge that they must have been highly vulnerable to hostile attack in those times. It is of local stone, as is the gatehouse with its Elizabethan half-timbered upper storey, and there is a moat, now dry and used as a garden. The castle escaped damage during the Civil War – Royalist cavalry sent to defend it retreated hastily – but the church was probably not so lucky, because it was extensively repaired in 1654, something that rarely happened during Cromwell's Protectorate. More work took place in 1664, the fourth year of Charles II's reign, and the wooden-roofed pulpit and squire's new probably date from this time. The gallery is Georgian, and there is a note on the organ below it that the band, which provided the church music until the 1850s, consisted of a bass viol, flute and clarinet.

In a long, narrow and tree-lined stretch just north of Craven Arms, the A49 follows the line of the Roman road, Watling Street West, as it runs from Leintwardine to the Stretton Gap. It veers off line by the time it crosses the Onny near the A489 junction, immediately opposite the entrance to what was a pleasant country house called The Grove. Now it is occupied by one of the biggest poultry producing plants in Britain. Through the gates come millions and millions of frozen chickens, bound for abroad as well as for consumption in this country. The firm, now owned by an international food empire, was started by four locally-born brothers and is one of the largest employers in South Shropshire. The old Roman road was probably pushed off route when the railway track was laid, but the Romans' dead-straight line remains as the lane through Wistanstow. The Saxons set up a church here to commemorate Saint Wystan, who was murdered in a dispute about whether he should succeed to the Mercian throne. Like many of the houses, including The Plough, which brews its own beer, the church is on the site of a Saxon predecessor. It has a strong tower dating back to the time of Richard the Lionheart, and a romantic story linked with it. According to South Shropshire District Council's guide book, centuries ago a local girl fell in love with a man who had wandered into the village and was thought to be a ne'er-do-well. After their marriage, he revealed himself to be the Marquis of Exeter – so the Wistanstow girl finished up as the Lady of Burghley House in Lincolnshire.

The prominent wooded escarpment eastwards from here, seen across what is known as Ape Dale, is Wenlock

175

Castle and gatehouse at Stokesay, from the churchyard

Edge, nearing the end of its seventeen-mile stretch from Much Wenlock. But the tower so visible against the skyline is not on its crest as appears, but on the highest point of an almost parallel range of limestone hills enclosing another valley, Hope Dale, that is so small there is not even a hamlet in it. The square tower, eighty feet high, is called Flounders' Folly, and the local story is that it was built by a man who plotted on the map that he would be able to see the Bristol Channel from it, but who committed suicide when he discovered that he had not taken into account a low hill in the foreground which blocked the view. In fact it was built in 1838 by a Mr Flounders to mark the spot where four landowners' boundaries met.

About three miles north on the A49, a minor road by an outstanding half-timbered house is signposted to Acton Scott and its Working Farm Museum. The Acton family, who have owned and lived on the estate since the thirteenth century, have put back the clock at their Home Farm. It is worked as it was in the times before the Motor Age, with shire horses providing the pulling power and traditional farm animals and poultry in the fields and buildings. With a working dairy and blacksmith's, wheelwright's and saddler's shops, it is open to the public except during winter months.

Back on the A49, a sudden kink over the Quinney Brook marks the entrance to the Stretton Gap, where ancient rock-faulting created a narrow corridor between two ranges of hills each more than one thousand million years old. Those to the west are the steep, rounded hills of the Longmynd, 1,695 feet at the highest point. To the east are the sharper, more individual volcanic hills that continue in almost a straight line across the Severn to The Wrekin, which is about 150 feet lower than the craggy Caer Caradoc that looms above Church Stretton, the second hill-fort in Shropshire, and at 1,506 feet the fifth highest.

Following the line the Roman engineers pioneered, the A49 bypasses Church Stretton and its outliers, Little Stretton and All Stretton, which are linked by the B4370, the main road until after the Second World War. A local story about the origin of their names is that King John, riding up from the south, came to a hamlet and asked what it was called. When told 'Stretton', he said that it was a little Stretton. Asking about the next, he was again told 'Stretton', and, seeing the Norman tower, said 'so this is Church Stretton'. When he had the same reply at the third, he commented: 'It is all Stretton about here.'

After a seventeenth-century attempt to turn a village into a market town had failed, Church Stretton was developed by Victorians who saw that it had many of the spa qualities of Malvern – invigorating air, hill country with plenty of walks, and pure water bubbling from springs. It became an established retirement place, particularly among officers who saw the hills as small-scale

All Saints, Little Stretton – Victorianism at its most exuberant, an eye-catching half-timbered church with a thatched roof

replicas of those in India. There are many black-and-white buildings, but all are less than a century old except the handful near the church and the tiny market square which stand near where Church Stretton's shopping streets meet. The church, built of a peculiar striped stone, has two sheila-na-gigs outside (much more weathered than the one at Kilpeck in Herefordshire). The nearby King's Arms and The Cottage (which used to be the Talbot Inn) have genuinely old half-timbered work.

From the crossroads at the town centre, a road to the top of the Longmynd crosses a cattle-grid and becomes a metalled, unfenced track giving a fantastic and fearsome view into the Cardingmill Valley, at the foot of the semi-precipitous hills. The easy way into the valley is along the road to All Stretton, taking a signposted lane that also gives access to the local golf club, the course of which on the hills above reaches 1,300 feet and challenges that at Kington as the highest in the country. Although the Cardingmill Valley is apt to be overrun by motorists at weekends, it can be a haven of peace, with a babbling stream and walks into the Longmynd valleys and to its challenging crest. Next best to it is Ashes Hollow at Little Stretton, which has just about the utmost in Victorian folksiness – a black-and-white church with a thatched roof. Amid deep-cut lanes further along the Longmynd is Minton, still shaped as it was in Saxon times, a cluster of houses and cottages rebuilt on sites more than a thousand years old around a central tump.

From Church Stretton's traffic lights on the A49, the B4371 climbs between Hazler Hill and craggy Caer Caradoc to wander across fertile farmland. It is the only road to dare the steep ascent of Wenlock Edge and then run along the crest to Much Wenlock past the quarries which still extract limestone containing vast quantities of the fossils of creatures that lived in the Silurian Sea 400 million years ago. From the road, lanes branch off to serve the ancient settlements and farmstead sites in Ape Dale – which probably derives from 'valley of the apples'. Footpaths to the tops of Caer Caradoc and The Lawley, to its north, are marked near tidy Hope Bowdler and Cardington, which in its layout is probably as old as Minton. In Cardington church is the tomb of Judge William Leighton, a chief justice of North Wales, who lived at nearby Plaish Hall, built in 1540 and probably the first brick mansion in Shropshire. Hughley, at the foot of the Edge, had a steeple attributed to its church by Housman although in reality it has a brick and half-timbered bellcote, with a clock presented by the Earl of Bradford after winning the 1892 Derby. Grand sounding Longville-in-the-Dale and Eaton-under-Heywood are little more than closely clustered farmsteads with a few houses, although the latter has a tucked-away thirteenth-century church containing an oak effigy probably more than 600 years old. Ticklerton is as small, but Rushbury is a village of great age, with a prehistoric mound near the Manor House that is surrounded by an earth bank still

179

ten feet high in places. The Norman church is believed to include stone that the Romans quarried and the Saxons reshaped, used in its predecessor. South-east of the village, at significantly named Roman Bank, is a path for which a stone packhorse bridge, six feet wide but with no parapets, was built across the Eaton Brook unknown centuries ago.

The largest of these South Shropshire dales is the most easterly, Corve Dale, with its fertile red earth that makes it some of the best farming land in Shropshire. The very old word 'corve' means 'a pass or cutting' (it is the same basic word as that of 'Corfe' Castle in Dorset), and it seems that the river's name comes from the valley it flows through. Turnpike commissioners laid new roads through it at the end of the eighteenth century, which explains the long straight stretches and why such villages as Culmington, Diddlebury and Stanton Long have no main roads through them.

Culmington stands near the junction of the River Corve and the Pye Brook (which drains the western slopes of the Brown Clee), about five miles out of Ludlow. Its church with its fourteenth-century unfinished tower was capped by an aluminium top in 1969, and has some Saxon her-ringbone masonry, as does Diddlebury just to the north. There, in the pathway at the church entrance, is a great millstone that must have been driven by the stream that flows through the village. Nearby Delbury Hall reveals the alternative spelling and pronunciation of the place-name.

The turnpike roads from Craven Arms and Ludlow, now the B4368, run along the west side of Corve Dale, through hamlets each with an inn from the coaching days. The stone and half-timbered Swan at Aston Munslow has a lane beside it which leads to The White House, open to the public during summer months as a country life museum. It dates back to at least Saxon times, with thirteenth-, fifteenth-, seventeenth-, and eighteenth-century additions, and has gardens on which artificial fertilizers have never been used. Among the plants grown is woad, from which the Britons extracted a blue juice to stain themselves before battle. At Munslow proper, half-a-mile on, the tucked-away Norman church has an unusual doorstop – a huge brick from the Great Wall of China, given in 1884.

About three miles further on, the B4368 swings east across Corve Dale for Morville and Bridgnorth, by-passing Stanton Long, where zealous Victorian restorers left the church with its original thirteenth-century door. Nearby is the deserted village of Holdgate, where the church that remains has a huge tower and a richly decorated Norman doorway. On the outside wall of the south chancel is a sheila-na-gig – but Tugford, a little way east, goes even further with these puzzling figures by having two of them, inside and left and right of the entrance door.

At Bouldon, a water wheel and grindstone near the local public house, the Tally Ho, are on the site of a mill

The Saxon-cum-Norman church at Diddlebury, seen across the old ford

mentioned in Domesday Book – in its time it produced flour, iron and paper. It was driven by the Clee Brook, which comes tumbling down from a broad shelf of hard rock that rises three hundred feet above the valley floor and runs for miles below the Brown Clee. It was able to support several villages, but now only two remain. Clee St Margaret, where the church has Saxon remains, is notable for one of the longest fords in the country – the Clee Brook runs for fifty yards down the main street over dhu-stone setts quarried from the Brown Clee which, rising above to a height of 1,792 feet, is the highest point in Shropshire. The quarrying removed all traces of the prehistoric camps on the twin summits of Clee Burf and Abdon Burf but traces remain of a third camp lower down, Nordy Bank. The other village is Stoke St Milborough, which perpetuates the name of St Milburga, a Saxon princess who, towards the end of the seventh century, became the first head of a newly established abbey at Much Wenlock. Near the parish church is a spring called St Milburga's Well, which is supposed to have burst out where her horse stumbled as she was being pursued by bloodhounds belonging to her enemies.

Hummocky ground indicates deserted villages near the churches at Cold Weston, Abdon and Heath. The two former were heavily restored by the Victorians, but Heath Chapel (it has no dedication) remains much as it was when the Normans completed it and is one of the finest survivals in the country of a simple, unrestored Norman church.

Where the Brown Clee fades away northwards is Ditton Priors. Here cottages built in the eighteenth and nineteenth centuries stretch out from an older village centre. The church has a shingled spire rather like Cleobury Mortimer's (but straight), and monuments inside include a brass tablet to a former vicar that is confusing to read because it has neither punctuation nor capital letters.

A typical Corve Dale lane downhill to Stanton Long runs back to the B4368 and its curve-away from the main road, the B4378, leading up the valley to Much Wenlock. It soon passes Shipton Hall (open to the public on Thursday afternoons in summer), which was rebuilt towards the end of the eighteenth century, and which has cast-iron fireplaces from Coalbrookdale. When that happened, the existing village was pulled down because it obscured the view and a new one built – which is why the church seems strangely set.

Tucked away in the wooded hills above is Wilderhope Manor, a late sixteenth-century house with rich plaster ceilings that belongs to the National Trust. It is used as a youth hostel, and is open to the public on Wednesday afternoons in summer. And in a road that leads to the top of Wenlock Edge is Easthope, where the sanctuary ring from the medieval church burnt down in 1927 has been fixed to the door of the replacement.

The narrow High Street at Much Wenlock, with half-timbered shops and a bank

Much Wenlock – where the B4371 and the B4372 converge by an old coaching inn called the Gaskell Arms – grew up to serve a religious community (as did St Albans and Bury St Edmunds), and not under the protection of a castle as so many Marcher towns did. As at Leominster, an early Saxon community was refounded before the Conquest by Earl Leofric, and Wenlock Abbey became enormously wealthy and a great landowner. The remains (cared for by the Department of the Environment), include the chapter house, which has interlaced Norman arcading within, and parts of the lavatorium, where the monks washed. The prior's lodge, dated about 1500, is one of the finest buildings of that time in the country.

Much Wenlock's parish church is unusually large because it had to serve a huge parish but was too extensively restored for there to be much to see. Its Norman tower dominates the nestle of narrow streets that converge on it and the Guildhall. This is Elizabethan, with the half-timbered upper storey mounted on huge wooden pillars now linked by iron railings that enclose what was the Butter Market. Inside are the town's stocks, mounted on small wheels so that they could be moved around. The richly timbered upper storey, which is open to the public, is still used for council meetings and magistrates' courts, although like so many other small towns, Much Wenlock lost its borough status in 1967.

On the opposite corner a museum is housed in what was the Market Hall. This was built in the 1850s, as was the Corn Market a little further up High Street, in which most of the town's best domestic buildings stand. They include two half-timbered fronts that bear the dates 1682 and 1693 – but these, like so many others in the street, conceal much older buildings 'modernized' down the centuries.

The 'Much' in the town's name is the only Shropshire example of the Herefordshire use of place names indicating the larger of two townships. Little Wenlock is on the other side of the Severn, on the slopes of The Wrekin. The link between them is the bridge at Buildwas, where monks from Furness Abbey in north-west England built an abbey about 1150. A footpath to its ruins (Department of the Environment) is signposted south of the present bridge – a post-war steel structure that conservationists regard as a calamity. It replaced the first cast-iron bridge designed by Thomas Telford in 1795 (after an older one was swept away by the Severn in flood) which incorporated his improvements on the design of the first iron bridge in the world, built seventeen years before, a couple of miles downriver. At 130 feet, its span was nearly a quarter more than the old bridge's, and it needed only 173 tons of iron compared with 378. The bridge has no footpath so care has to be taken when admiring the view, particularly that to the entrance to the Severn Gorge. There, on the south bank, is an example of modern engineering – the cooling towers of the Buildwas

Looking east to the chancel in the remains of Buildwas Abbey, on the banks of the Severn

electricity generating stations. On the north are the Coalbrookdale furnaces, where the Industrial Revolution began. If they could see it all now, the gorge's iron-masters would be proud.

Index

188

INDEX